GO[D]

ISN[']T

FINISHED

WITH ME

YET

GOD

ISN'T

FINISHED

WITH ME

YET

**DISCOVERING THE SPIRITUAL
GRACES OF LATER LIFE**

BARBARA LEE

LOYOLA PRESS.
A JESUIT MINISTRY
Chicago

LOYOLA PRESS.
A JESUIT MINISTRY

3441 N. Ashland Avenue
Chicago, Illinois 60657
(800) 621-1008
www.loyolapress.com

Scriptural references, unless otherwise specified, are from the *New American Bible*, revised edition © 2008, 1991, 1986, 1970 Confraternity of Christian Doctrine, Inc. Washington DC. All rights reserved.

Quotations from the *Spiritual Exercises of St. Ignatius Loyola* are from the Ganss edition, *Ignatius of Loyola: Spiritual Exercises and Selected Works*, ed. George E. Ganss, SJ (Mahwah, NJ: Paulist Press, 1991). I have followed the standard practice of citing the Exercises by paragraph number rather than by the page on which they appear in any particular published edition. For example, Ignatius's guidelines for making certain kinds of decisions are cited SpEx 179–183, or simply 179–183.

Quotations from the autobiography of St. Ignatius are from the translation by Parmananda R. Divarkar, SJ, *A Pilgrim's Testament: The Memoirs of Saint Ignatius of Loyola* (1983). As with the Spiritual Exercises, I have followed the convention of citing by paragraph number.

Portions of this book first appeared in "Faith in Focus: Aging with Ignatius (Applying the Spiritual Exercises in the Later Stages of Life)" *America*, Vol. 214 No. 11, March 28, 2016, pp. 27–29.

To protect the privacy of those who shared their stories in chapters 2 and 4, I have used middle names or pseudonyms.

Cover art credit: Irina Guseva/iStock/Thinkstock
Back cover author photo, Rebecca Pearson.

ISBN: 978-0-8294-4661-6
Library of Congress Control Number: 2017962525

Printed in the United States of America.
17 18 19 20 21 22 23 24 25 26 27 Versa 10 9 8 7 6 5 4 3 2 1

Contents

1

Finding God in All Things

In the late 1970s, the parish council of which I was a member undertook a survey of parishioners' interests and needs. Our objectives were to identify unmet needs and to improve existing parish organizations and services. One woman responded with a single sentence: "I am eighty-six years old, and my opinions don't matter."

That one sentence contained a multitude of issues:

- the marginalization of older adults
- the way they have internalized the attitudes that cause it
- their lack of a voice, and, above all,
- the existence of these conditions in a parish context

I began asking questions:

- Where are the guideposts for the spiritual life of the aging?
- What does Christian spirituality offer to counter the secular literature on decline, diminishment, and death?
- Is anybody telling an eighty-six-year-old woman that her opinions *do* matter?

I only gradually began to find some answers as I myself aged.

My Story: Why This Book?

When I retired after a rewarding career as a lawyer and a judge, I discovered that I had become invisible. As a litigation partner in a law firm at a time when women were still a small minority in the field of law, I was recognizable. As a judge, I received respectful deference, sometimes excessively so, from the lawyers who practiced before me. Suddenly, for the first time in my adult life, it was Monday morning and I had no appointments—nobody awaiting my arrival; nobody calling my still-unlisted telephone number. As an only child who never married, I could not take convenient refuge in "spending more time with the family." I had to address the question, *Who am I now?*

In 1962, I was one of sixteen women in a Harvard Law School graduating class of 468. Harvard had been the last major law school to admit women, in 1950, and in the early sixties there were still professors who explained at length why it had been a bad idea. The reason most often given was that we were taking up places in the class that would otherwise have gone to men who would "use" their legal education. (The sixteen women in my graduating class include three judges and four law professors.) Some of the older faculty complained that now they were required to clean up their language. It took a strong sense of self to compete in that environment. The answer to "Who am I?" was clear. I saw myself as a lawyer and as a person who knew how to succeed in a competitive, even hostile, environment. After graduation, the challenges were greater: laws prohibiting discrimination based on sex did not exist prior to the Civil Rights Act of 1964, and that law was not widely enforced for another decade after that. I persevered because I truly believed that this was my vocation.

During much of my career, I often felt that I had one foot in each of two worlds. I worked in an aggressively secular environment, among people who did not share my values. At the same time, I was active in parish and ecumenical activities among religious people who had no concept of my professional life or the special pressures it involved. By the time I was in my early forties, I was searching for a way to integrate these two ways of living. My spiritual director at the time recommended that I make the Spiritual Exercises of St. Ignatius. I did so in the form known as The Retreat in Daily Life (also known as The Nineteenth Annotation). Over an eight-month period, I met weekly with my director and under her guidance followed a prayer schedule in accordance with Ignatius's schematic, including Scripture reading and journaling. In the course of "making" the Exercises, I learned something about decision making and how to pray with Scripture, both of which I will discuss in detail later in this book. I also acquired a better understanding of my vocation. When my director asked if I could summarize in a sentence what the Exercises meant for me, I said, quoting an older translation of St. Paul: "I live, yet not I, but Christ lives in me" (Gal. 2:20).

All things happen in God's time. A few months after I completed the Exercises, the law firm of which I was a partner dissolved because of a conflict between the two principal partners. I was "downsized" before the word was in my vocabulary. Who was I? No longer a partner in a law firm, I still defined myself as a lawyer and a person who knew how to succeed in a competitive environment. Applying what I had learned about prayerful decision making, I decided to open my own office. I saw a chance, as a solo practitioner, to better integrate the two worlds in which I was living—for example, by taking on more *pro bono* work than had been possible in my former situation. Among other things, I represented a not-for-profit organization, which I billed at a reduced rate or not at all—options that would not have been approved at my previous firm. I now had the freedom to do something new.

With the freedom came new challenges. I had to spend a great deal of time on client development and office management rather than on actual billable work. Not all clients paid promptly, but the rent, my secretary's salary, and all the other necessary office expenses nevertheless had to be met. Today there are a number of bar association programs and other resources for lawyers in these circumstances, but in the 1980s there was no playbook. I was on my own. I had to make choices about what to spend money on and how to allocate my time. I gained a new appreciation for these resources and the fact that all were gifts of God, to be used in love and service.

After five years of what I called my "desert period," I became a U.S. Magistrate Judge. Life could not have been more different. At the very beginning, an older judge gave me some advice that I think applies in life as much as in court. He said, "You can't change all the injustice that you see. All you can do is try to do justice in the individual case before you." That wisdom now seems to me to extend to the spiritual life: All we can do is live in the present moment and try to find the grace in it.

After retirement, I found myself asking again, "Who am I now?" The Holy Spirit began moving me toward answers.

A neighbor of mine was one of the original members of the Ignatian Lay Volunteer Corps (as it was then called), an organization of retired adults who do volunteer work among the poor in the context of Ignatian spirituality.[1] I sent for an application but hesitated over the requirement of two days a week for ten months of the year. My ninety-year-old mother was in assisted living in Connecticut, and managing her affairs required a lot of my time. I set the application aside for future reference. A year and a half later, and barely weeks after my mother died, I received a call from the regional coordinator for the New York area, who said she was going through old files and wanted to know whether I was still interested. I said I was and asked for a new set of application materials. When they arrived, I was busy with other things, and I set them aside. She called *again*! Putting myself in her place, I knew I would never have had the courage to do that. I realized that when I hadn't responded to the whisper, the Holy Spirit raised her voice.

I became an Ignatian Volunteer in September 2000. I was placed on Manhattan's Lower East Side at Cabrini Immigrant Services, a new organization that needed volunteer English teachers.[2] On paper, I had no official qualifications for this task, but it seemed right. The director was a practical woman who put more emphasis on character and commitment than on formal qualifications. With a lot of research and help from experienced teachers, I began teaching an intermediate-level English class for mostly Chinese immigrants.

That first class of students taught me how to teach. I learned their needs and found ways to address them. They also taught me a lot about lifelong learning. The ability to learn a second language falls off sharply after childhood, and for mature adults it's hard work. Some of my students over the years have been older than I am, shining examples of what older people can accomplish.

But my story does not end there. After sixteen grace-filled years teaching English and a long period of discernment, I have, at age eighty, embarked on a new ministry as a spiritual director. To qualify, I spent three summers at Creighton University's Graduate School of Theology, where I was by far the oldest student in an internationally and ecumenically diverse class. I expected from the beginning that once I was fully certified, I would be working with people in my own age group, particularly with other Ignatian Volunteers. However, for my practicum (the Latin name for the internship between the second and third summers), I found myself guiding four people in their early twenties. I am reminded of a Jewish proverb to the effect that we make our plans, and God laughs.[3] I also worried that in light of the supposed short attention spans of millennials, one or more of them would drop out, jeopardizing my ability to satisfy the practicum requirement. To my great joy (and immense relief), they all stayed the course for the full nine-month commitment, and I learned a great deal about how the Holy Spirit moves both director and directee.

Reflecting on these experiences in the context of Ignatian spirituality, I have come to a whole new way of looking at the Christian vocation of older adults.

For those of us who grew up before the Second Vatican Council, *vocation* had a very narrow meaning: A person who "had a vocation" was going to be a priest or a nun and was called upon to make a lifetime commitment. Today we have a much broader understanding of what it means to live the gospel, to share the Good News. The Holy Spirit has breathed life into some creative new forms of vocation. Some of the better-known organizations are the Jesuit Volunteer

Corps, which invites recent college graduates to live in community for a year while doing full-time volunteer service[4]; Mercy Associates, a similar program of the Sisters of Mercy[5]; Jean Vanier's L'Arche Communities, whose volunteers live in community for a year or two with people who are developmentally disabled[6]; and, of course, my own group, Ignatian Volunteer Corps, whose members commit from year to year for two days a week, September to June. These and many others invite laypeople to give some of their time and talent at specific times in their life's journey to pray together and to serve those in need.

My experience as an Ignatian Volunteer has led me to understand that those of us who have retired from full-time paid work have entered a new stage of life—a new kind of vocation, with a unique charism. Not everyone has the ability or the opportunity to do volunteer work, but we can all experience the graces particular to this stage of life. Ignatian spirituality, particularly as reflected in some of the forms of prayer discussed in this book, can open us to those graces.

Older adults are in several ways a spiritually underserved population. Many parishes have a variety of programs for children, teens, and families but make no effort to address the aging apart from the general sacramental life of the congregation. A woman I interviewed in the course of writing this book complained that a campaign to make her parish more responsive to the needs of older members resulted in the addition of bus trips for seniors but nothing with a spiritual dimension. The chapters that follow will discuss the spiritual dimensions of some of the transitions that occur as we age: retirement, empty nesting, caregiving, and various kinds of losses.

Your Story: Is This Book for You?

When the Social Security Act was passed in 1935, Congress fixed sixty-five as the normal retirement age because the average life expectancy was short. A sixty-five-year-old was *old*. That is certainly no longer true. Older Americans are an increasing percentage of the population, and we are living longer than ever. In 2014, the latest year for which statistics are available, there were approximately 46.2 million people over age 65 (14.5 percent of the population), 6.2 million over 85, and more than 72,000 people age 100 or older.[7] Yet our youth-conscious society has not caught up with this new reality. Television commercials aimed at our age group give the impression that older adults spend most of their time talking to their doctors, with occasional breaks to plant flowers, walk the dog, and explain at great length how they stopped smoking. *That's not who we are!*

This book is for the aging. I won't attempt to define "aging" in years. We are all aging from the day we are born. Many people lead active, productive lives in their eighties and nineties; some people feel "old" in their fifties. Nor is it very helpful to speak of "senior citizens," a ubiquitous phrase with a condescending undertone. The people I have met who have experienced an identity crisis similar to mine cover a wide range of ages. They include, among others, the newly retired (voluntarily or not); those contemplating retirement; empty-nest parents; those who have experienced a sudden sense of mortality due to a health crisis or the loss of a loved one; and anyone who feels that more of life is behind than ahead. If you relate to one of those descriptions, please read on.

This book is for Christians, especially—but not only—Catholics, who want to grow in a God-centered life by exploring the graces specific to the later stages of life. It is grounded in the Spiritual Exercises of St. Ignatius of Loyola and the rich tradition derived from them. This approach to the spiritual life will be familiar to some readers and new to others. A brief introduction to Ignatian spirituality will help define the context for both groups of readers.

Introduction to Ignatian Spirituality

Ignatius of Loyola (1491–1556) was trained for court life in imperial Spain. Later he served as a soldier and appears to have fully enjoyed the pleasures available to an ambitious young man of his social class. Religion had only superficial importance for him until, at the age of thirty, he was seriously injured in battle. Facing a long, painful recuperation with nothing to read except the lives of the saints and a book on the life of Christ, he began to reflect on his feelings: What caused him to feel peaceful; what left him dry and agitated? These meditations led him deeper into the spiritual life and eventually to a new definition of who he was and who he was called to be: spiritual teacher and, eventually, founder of the Society of Jesus.

Ignatius is best known for the Spiritual Exercises. They were originally designed to be experienced in a retreat setting over a thirty-day period of intense prayer, meditation, and silence. This is still a common practice, especially for Jesuits. For people who could not remove themselves from their everyday responsibilities for such a continuous period, Ignatius suggested adaptations. Of these, the best known is The Retreat in Daily Life (also called The Nineteenth Annotation), which involves a commitment to regular prayer over an extended period. Ignatius's annotations to the Exercises also recommended a simplified version intended for people unable because of age or disability to make the full retreat.[8] Today, the key principles of the Exercises have been adapted by many spiritual directors in different contexts, such as eight-day directed retreats; parish programs offering abbreviated versions of The Retreat in Daily Life; and online retreats in various languages and formats, including the full Exercises and guidelines for groups. For those who may be interested in making the full Exercises or in pursuing a retreat or a parish program, I have provided links to some resources in Ignatian Resources at the end of the book.

The Exercises are intended as an experience to be lived, not a book to be read. Ignatius wrote the text specifically for spiritual directors, not for the people they direct. *God Isn't Finished with Me Yet* is neither a comprehensive study of Ignatian spirituality nor a path through the Exercises. This book explores the wisdom in the Exercises that has much broader application.

First and foremost, the Exercises are about encountering, loving, and following Jesus.[9] We are encouraged to see everything in our lives as a means to this end. At the outset, we are asked to make a conscious choice that moves us away from self-absorption and toward a God-centered life. Ignatius prescribed meditations on creation, on sin, on God's boundless love for us as sinners, and above all, on the life, ministry, sufferings, and death of Jesus. In both the full Exercises and its various adaptations, the retreatant prays with Scripture, examines his or her own responses, records them in a journal, and learns to discern the difference between the promptings of the Holy Spirit and the impulses that come from other sources. The common thread throughout is *finding God in all things*.

This was not an entirely new idea in Ignatius's time. His contribution was to expand the idea of "all things" beyond traditional ideas such as the beauty of nature and the happenstances of life. Ignatius's great insight was that God is present in our emotions, our imagination, our memories—indeed, in the deepest parts of our being. Much of Ignatian spirituality is directed to recognizing the subtle ways in which God is revealed to us deep within ourselves.

The chapters that follow will discuss how Ignatius's advice on prayer, decision making, and discernment can provide guidance for some of the challenges faced by older adults. But this book is not a recruiting tool for any particular program or form of prayer. It is an invitation to companionship on the spiritual journey. There is still a great deal of the road ahead, at any age. *God isn't finished with us yet!*

Prayer Exercise: Living in the Present

Those of us who have been blessed with long lives have a great store of memories. We also may worry about the future, no matter how well we have planned for it. To be open to God's grace in the present, we need to deepen our awareness of the present.

Find a comfortable place to sit, in an area where there is some activity but not excessive noise: a park bench, an outdoor café during an off-peak time, a mall, or even your own front porch, if you are lucky enough to have one. Shut off your phone. Relax, breathe deeply, and acknowledge God's presence.

Begin to notice your surroundings. What is the composition of the seat you're sitting on and the structures around you: wood, metal, concrete, glass, marble, plastic? Notice the texture, the colors, the shapes and sizes. What is the air around you like: warm, cool, windy, humid? What can you hear: traffic, voices, music? Are there odors, scents?

Next, notice the people. Without staring, observe if they are alone or in groups, adults or children. Are they walking purposefully or strolling? What does their body language tell you about where they may be going or how they may be feeling? Are they relaxed, tense?

Focus on your own feelings. Are you comfortable? Relaxed? Why or why not?

When you are ready, thank God for the experience.

2

Identity: Who Am I Now?

To begin, ask yourself this question:

What do I do?

When you meet someone for the first time at a party, a parish event, or any other situation in which strangers make small talk, this is the first question most people ask. We have different answers at different times in our lives: *I'm in graduate school; I'm a teacher; I'm a telecommuter; I've just started my own business or opened my own law office.* The conversation proceeds—or not—from there. The exchange is so well accepted as an icebreaker in American society that we ask and answer it almost automatically, without reflecting on how it defines us. Yet the cultural assumption that *we are what we do* becomes more obvious—sometimes painfully so—as we age. Transitions such as retirement, the empty-nest experience, caregiving responsibilities, and losses of various kinds prompt many older adults to ask not *What do I do?* but *Who am I?*

Once we cease to find our identity in how we earn our living, we can discover new paths to self-examination and spiritual growth.

Retirement

For many of us in twenty-first-century America, particularly those in skilled professional or management positions, identity is bound up with our work. Retirement, even when planned, can thus be a shock. That was certainly my experience. I was suddenly an invisible woman in late middle age. Lawyers I encountered at bar-association functions didn't always remember who I was. Friends who were still working were on a different wavelength. My volunteer work in the parish and other religious organizations was ongoing, and I was a part-time caregiver for my mother, but none of these roles was identity defining.

Even as the retirement age edges up in the United States, both men and women are spending more years in retirement. The question of identity at this stage of life is therefore not trivial.

Various studies have demonstrated that women live longer in retirement than men do. This may follow women's greater longevity in general, but only in part. We all know, or have heard stories about, men who retired from satisfying careers and were dead within the year. Would the heart attack or the cancer have struck while they were still working? Or do some men adjust poorly to retirement because they have been so totally invested in their working selves?

As recently as fifty years ago, this problem was mostly limited to men, because men were the breadwinners and women who worked at all were often restricted to menial, low-paying jobs. But the baby boomer generation—those born during the post-World War II spike in the birth rate—came of age when opportunities for women were opening up. This age group includes the first wave of successful professional and businesswomen. Their ranks continue to grow. While there are no statistics showing how this change may have affected women's longevity after retirement, one thing is clear: A definition of self that is tied up in work is no longer a single-gender phenomenon.

The first Monday morning after retirement is a moment of truth for many people: no place where you are expected to be; no urgent telephone calls; nobody depending on you. The experience can be devastating for anyone whose retirement was not voluntary. Even people whose retirement date has been carefully planned and chosen may be shocked at the magnitude of the change. Work provided a structure that now is lacking, a social network to which you no longer belong, and intellectual stimulation for which television, golf, and grandchildren are not adequate substitutes. Loneliness is a common experience, whether expressed or not. For some people, depression ensues.

Retirement can be life changing for family members as well. Many women describe the disruptive effect of a newly-retired husband who is suddenly home all day. For both spouses, "Who am I now?" may entail reexamining their relationship and considering the unstated assumptions of a lifetime.

Then there are the grandchildren. A common refrain of people about to retire is, "I'll get to spend more time with my grandchildren!" Sometimes this is wonderful, but sometimes the busy parents of small children are all too eager to define *grandparent* as "babysitter." It's hard to say no, but for many grandparents the question becomes: Is this who I am now—a babysitter?

A life-threatening illness in retirement can pose even more painful questions of identity.

Joseph, CEO of a successful business, planned his retirement well in advance. He and his wife decided to move to New York City. In addition to spending time with family and embarking on the leisure travel he had long waited to do, he had two goals for life after retirement: learn something new and "give back" some of the blessings he had enjoyed. He found the opportunity for both in a program helping people transition out of homelessness. As he watched people he had mentored graduate from the program, he felt that what he was doing really mattered. His eyes had been opened to what life is like for people who are poor. He was also learning the principles and practices of Ignatian spirituality. Joseph felt good about where his life was going. Then he was diagnosed with prostate cancer.

He researched his options—a complicated process—and finally decided on surgery. Joseph felt fortunate that his cancer was caught early; that he had health insurance and a supportive wife and family; and that he lived in a city where outstanding medical care was available. The surgery was successful, and Joseph went back to volunteer work for eighteen months. Then the cancer returned.

This time the treatment was a three-month course of intensive radiation therapy. This, too, was successful. Again Joseph was grateful, especially for the fact that he was otherwise in good health and did not have to worry about the complications that often affect people in their sixties who have multiple medical problems.

A year later, another test came back positive. Because the reading was very low, his oncologist recommended frequent testing, watching, and waiting. Joseph found himself facing new decisions about what to do during this period of uncertainty. What he decided was that he would not be defined by cancer. He has known people, including a member of his own family, whose identity was overwhelmed by the disease, and he is determined not to let that happen to him. He believes that Ignatian spirituality helped light the way.

Empty Nest

Many women, regardless of the kind of work they do, define themselves primarily in terms of relationships: John's wife, Betty's mother, somebody's caregiver. There is a long cultural tradition conditioning us to this way of thinking. As recently as the nineteenth century, in many states, married women could not own property. Prior to the Civil Rights Act of 1964, many employers refused to hire women with small children. Pregnant teachers and flight attendants, among others, were expected to quit their jobs as soon as their condition was known. The Roman Catholic Church in many ways contributed to this kind of pigeonholing: before Pope John Paul II greatly expanded the number and diversity of canonized saints, almost all women saints in the Roman calendar were either "virgin" or "martyr"; there did not appear to be any other recognized path to sanctity for women.

Despite changes in attitude, many women experience an identity crisis when their adult children leave home. Feelings of loneliness can be acute. If a husband is still working, or has died, a large, empty house or apartment can be oppressive.

Rosa is the single mother of an adopted daughter. Middle-aged when she adopted, she is now retired from a successful professional career and faces her daughter's departure from home at a particularly vulnerable time. Complicating her transition is the likelihood that her daughter will move to the opposite coast to pursue a career in a highly specialized field centered there. For Rosa, "Who am I now?" is a question about filling the suddenly empty spaces in what had been a rich and generous life. Prayer is more important to her than ever.

Caregiving

As average life expectancy increases, so do the numbers of people in their eighties and nineties—the age group most likely to need help caring for themselves as they age. Often the caregiver is a daughter (or daughter-in-law) who is herself past age sixty-five, or a wife who has her own physical limitations. It is a harsh reality for many women—because caregivers are overwhelmingly women—that they must take on the arduous role of caregiver at just the point in their lives when they need to take better care of themselves. Sometimes the burden is physical: the household must revolve around the needs of a disabled spouse or parent, and there is a lot of (literal) heavy lifting. There are additional challenges when a patient who is cognitively impaired cannot be left alone or when a terminal illness leads to intense emotional stress. For many people, the question inevitably arises: Is my husband (or wife or father or mother or brother) better off in a nursing home? Many people who could remain in their own homes with a certain amount of skilled nursing and other assistance are forced into institutions by rigid Medicare and Medicaid rules. Sometimes there is no realistic choice, but that doesn't make it easy. The caregiver's own health may suffer if she continues to keep her loved one at home.

Parents of a special-needs child who may outlive them face unique challenges. Elizabeth was the CEO of a large not-for-profit organization. She and her husband, also a hard-working professional, had four children, one of whom has Down syndrome. For most of his life, they were able to arrange their schedules so that they could keep him with them. When Elizabeth's husband of forty years died, this was no longer possible. Soon thereafter, she retired from her job at age seventy-five, moved back to her hometown, and found a group home for her son not far away. Although she brings him home every other weekend and his siblings visit, he is not happy. He told her, "This isn't home. They don't love me here." She is torn by the pain she feels at his unhappiness and the desire to bring him to live with her. Yet she knows that at age eighty, this is not a realistic solution, not only because she may not be able to care for him but because he will have yet another difficult transition when she dies.

Those who work in the helping professions may have different challenges in transition. Marilyn felt called to the contemplative life as a young woman but did not follow through. She trained as a nurse, rose to supervisory positions with major responsibilities, married, and raised three children while working part-time. When her children were grown, she went back to full-time work, glad for the opportunity to set aside a little money for "old age." Then her husband was diagnosed with a terminal illness. She left her job to become a caregiver for what she describes as the "long and difficult last couple of years" of her husband's life. After his death, she went back to work part-time. This new stage of her life was interrupted by a serious accident. The first responders who pulled her from the car initially thought she was dead. There followed a long and painful convalescence, in which she was no longer a caregiver but a person in need of care. As a nurse, she found this especially difficult, hearing the cries of other patients in need of help. Now recovered, she lives alone in her own apartment and says that she has "landed in a place where I can begin to live a contemplative life."

Losses

Widows and widowers face particularly painful transitions. The disorientation of retirement, the loneliness of the empty nest, and the stresses of caregiving are often exacerbated by the loss of a spouse. For many women, the immediate concern is financial: Is there enough to live on without the husband's earnings or pension? For men, the question is often "Who is going to take care of me?" For both men and women, the loss of a life partner can seem like the amputation of part of oneself.

Edward is an eighty-two-year-old widower with no children. When his wife died a few years ago, he found it too painful to remain in the apartment they had shared. Within five months, he had moved to a retirement community. As he put it, he then "had to come to grips with how to maximize the time I have left." Edward is healthy enough for independent living and until recently did volunteer work two days a week. He still tries to help others, such as offering rides to those who can no longer drive, and he describes himself as becoming "more faith-oriented and more spiritual" in the years that he has been alone.

Some losses are less foreseeable. Matilda was a widow in her seventies, in good health, living in her own home, driving her own car, and socializing with friends. She particularly enjoyed serving as an officer of a retirees' group sponsored by the company where she had worked for many years. She took trips to nearby attractions, often with friends who were no longer able to drive. Despite her active lifestyle, her only son, who lived in a distant state and rarely visited, began to express concern about her living alone as she got older. After a lot of discussion, he persuaded her that she should move in with his family, with the promise of renovating their basement to make an apartment for her.

After Matilda sold her house and made the move, she found the reality quite different. It seemed that the appropriate permits could not be obtained for the proposed renovation, so she was relegated to a small bedroom on the second floor. It was so small, in fact, that the television set she had brought from home didn't fit and was given to her grandson. The family lived in a suburban area without public transportation. Soon after Matilda moved in, her car broke down and, for reasons that were never made clear, could not be repaired. It was the 1990s, before smartphones, and Matilda lost touch with many of her friends. She felt completely isolated. Yet, for the rest of her life, she never blamed or criticized her son.

There are other losses that often seem to go to the core of who we are. Sooner or later, age brings diminished capacity in one form or another. It may be gradual—loss of energy, need for a cane or a hearing aid—or it may be serious enough to lead to loss of independence. We can see these as forms of poverty unrelated to money or property. They can also entail loneliness, because the experiences cannot be shared by those who have not experienced them.

In all these situations, it is easy to focus on what is lost. It isn't easy to see widowhood or loss of the ability to drive as a call—much less a gift—from God. Yet there is grace in all these losses, all these transitions, and there is much in Ignatian spirituality that can help us experience the grace.

Ignatian Prayer: The Examen

Although Ignatius's sixteenth-century vocabulary would not have included a phrase such as *identity crisis*, the approach to prayer that he developed is well suited to the kind of self-questioning that comes at major turning points in life.

Ignatius applied these insights to, among other things, praying with Scripture, making decisions, and adopting a form of daily prayer designed to examine these experiences in detail. All these approaches to prayer can be especially meaningful to the aging. We begin by looking at the daily examination, which is central to Ignatian spirituality.

Discussions of Ignatian prayer almost always begin with the *examen*, a daily examination, or review, of one's immediate experience of the spiritual life. Originally, Ignatius prescribed an examination of conscience that focused on sin:

1. Give thanks.

2. Ask for the grace to know my sins.

3. Review the day in detail.

4. Ask pardon.

5. Resolve to amend.

Most of us who have a regular prayer life do not find serious sin, or even material for confession, in every single day's activities. In practice, Ignatius's five points soon extended to more positive reflections: not only on sin, but also on ways to grow in grace.

As the prayer has evolved, modern spiritual writers have moved away from the label *examination of conscience* in favor of descriptions that more accurately convey its positive emphasis. For example, Margaret Silf calls it the "Review Prayer,"[10] and Armand Nigro, SJ, uses the term "Awareness exercise." One of the most widely used terms is "Examination of Consciousness," coined by George Aschenbrenner, SJ.[11] I will follow the modern consensus, which favors *examen*, the original Spanish word, borrowed from Latin, that meant both "conscience" and "consciousness." Apart from simplicity, this title carries no preconceptions. The scope of the prayer is discovered by praying it.

Many modern spiritual guides recommend a kind of preface focusing first on the presence of God before the five traditional steps. After that, a typical five-point meditation might be the following:

1. Give thanks.

2. Ask for the light of the Spirit, to be aware of all the ways God is at work in my life.

3. Review the day, looking not only for my sins and failings but also for where I have heard the promptings of the Spirit and how I have responded.

4. Ask pardon for the ways in which I have failed to respond to grace.

5. Finally, ask for the grace not merely to amend my faults but also to look forward to the future with hope.

There is a good deal of literature on adapting Ignatius's bare-bones outline to the very different culture of our own times, as well as to specific circumstances. Some resources on the subject are included in Ignatian Resources. The outline that follows reflects the way I try to pray the *examen*. Most readers will find a rhythm and structure that best suits them.

Presence

The presence of God is the starting point for almost any form of prayer. We were taught as children to say, "I adore you, Jesus, present in the Blessed Sacrament" when arriving in church. Many prayers begin, "God, come to my assistance; Lord, make haste to help me." The *examen* is no exception.

I usually begin, "Lord, help me to be fully present for prayer." God's presence is only one side of this relationship. My presence is also necessary. I am not fully present if my prayer is distracted by anxiety or stress; if reflections on particular events of the preceding day cause me to detour into daydreaming; or if my mind races ahead to what I'm going to do next.

The next part of my prayer is "Lord, help me remember that I am always in your presence." I need to remind myself constantly that I meet God not only at Mass or in my times of formal prayer but wherever I go, whatever I do, and in whatever I happen to be thinking about. Sometimes this prayer step reminds me of a specific experience in which I have recognized God's presence, such as being on the receiving end of an unexpected kindness or hearing the day's Gospel in a particularly personal way. In the absence of such prompts, I try to focus my imagination on where God's presence is accessible: in the dawn of a new day (even a cold and rainy one); in the call of the mourning doves who have built a nest on the roof of a nearby building (even in midtown Manhattan we hear birdsong!); in all the good people in my life.

Thanksgiving

"Lord, thank you for all your generous gifts. Thank you for life and health and energy and opportunity. Thank you for all the gifts I take for granted and for all the blessings of this past day."

That is my usual general beginning. Life and health are no mere abstractions. I can never forget the friends of my youth who died too young or others whose later years have been diminished by disability. Every day is a gift. Every day is different. I try to focus first on one or more long-range gifts; some of my favorites are "Thank you that I can afford to live as I do without working for pay"; "Thank you that I am healthier than a great many people my age"; "Thank you for every beat of my heart and every breath I take." Then I review the preceding twenty-four hours to thank God for the gifts unique to that day, such as a friend I had lunch with, a thoughtful gift one of my students brought me from China, a perfect New York bagel.

Sometimes, instead of a detailed review, I ask myself, *For what am I most grateful today?* It may be one of those more permanent gifts or a small thing that went almost unnoticed. I hold it in my heart and lift it up to God.

The Light of the Spirit

"Lord, send your good Spirit to guide me." The insights that come in prayer are not our own doing. All is grace. The preceding step in the exercise will have reminded us that the very desire to pray is God's gift, as is everything that follows from it. We can neither demand nor deserve it. What we can do is acknowledge that all the insights in prayer are gifts of the Holy Spirit and attempt to be as receptive as possible.

Some spiritual writers place this prayer first, even before thanksgiving.[12] This approach invokes the aid of the Holy Spirit in exploring what we are thankful for. We all have days when it's a little more difficult to give thanks. At other times, gratitude may well up in us so that we cannot do otherwise than begin with thanks.

Review of the Day

Of all the steps in the *examen*, this is probably the one that needs the most practice. Reviewing the events of our day, either to thank God or to know our sins, is familiar enough. Reviewing the *feelings* that those events generate is a new approach for many people. A good way to begin is "Lord, where have I heard your voice, and how have I responded?"

Sometimes a strong emotion immediately surfaces. I was deeply saddened to get a letter from the son of an old friend telling me of her death. I was furious with the taxi driver who insisted on dropping me off four blocks from my destination. Emotions are not a matter of choice, but how we react to them is. Do I thank God for Kathy's friendship? Can I convey that gratitude in a letter of condolence to her son? Why was I so furious with the taxi driver? Did this trivial occurrence trigger some deeper anger that I have not identified or addressed? What do I want to say to God about these feelings? Can I listen to what God is saying to me?

Sometimes the prayer reveals responses to grace that may surprise us. On a recent opera tour, the woman sitting next to me—whom I had met the day before but did not know well—asked me three times whether the opera we were seeing was a new production. The second time, I was surprised to feel compassion well up in me as I realized what had caused her to keep repeating the question. Not long ago, I might have been merely annoyed. While there is no way to explain a grace of this kind, the practice of the *examen* illuminates God's gifts and, I believe, makes us readier to respond.

At other times, we may be given the grace to see how God is present in ways that differ from our expectations.

The composition of my English class has changed from year to year. Some years, there have been highly motivated people, eager to improve their English so they could pass the citizenship exam or get better jobs. At other times, the class has consisted mainly of older women who seemed more interested in socializing than in improving their fluency. My frustration and disappointment with the latter group surfaced during the *examen*, and I realized that I was concentrating on what I wanted from the experience rather than on what my students needed. In an immigrant community, social bonds are extremely important. My class *was* meeting a need—just not the one I was focused on.

Recently I made a long-anticipated pilgrimage to the Holy Land. I embarked full of eagerness for all the graces such a journey could entail. I was especially looking forward to the projected stops at Magdala and Bethany, because Mary Magdalene is special to me. A few small things went wrong at the beginning of the trip, which did not put me in the best possible frame of mind for what happened next. I got sick and missed a day and a half of the itinerary, including both Magdala and Bethany. I was bitterly disappointed; in fact, I felt cheated and told God so in prayer. Praying in front of the life-size crucifix at the Notre Dame of Jerusalem Center, I got an answer that was unmistakably clear: *Why do you expect Me to live up to your expectations? Who are you to tell Me what graces you should experience on this journey?* This was a lesson in humility, for one thing, and in discernment, for another. These were the graces of the pilgrimage, graces I am still unpacking many months later.

These examples are merely suggestive; there are many ways to reflect on feelings. But this part of the prayer should not be limited to the most powerful emotions of the day. It is important to review the day in more detail, searching for the subtler indications of what may be going on below the surface.

Some of my directees complain that they cannot focus on prayer, or on the *examen* in particular, because of "distractions." When I ask for examples of the distractions, the response is often pressure at work or a family issue. Important matters like these are not distractions; they are where God is for this person at this time, and they should become the subject of the prayer, at least part of the time. Real distractions are those that occur when we allow our minds to wander off to daydreams or focus on physical discomfort or on what someone else in the room or the church may be doing. In those circumstances, it's always a good idea to gently redirect our attention back to the prayer. But perhaps we shouldn't stop there. We might ask ourselves what we were praying about when the distraction occurred—is there an issue we don't want to face? However, when the distractions, particularly recurring ones, relate to important aspects of our lives, they should be recognized as indications of our deeper feelings and, as such, signposts pointing to material for prayer and discernment.

Even the most mundane events can reveal the presence of grace and the call to respond. All that is required is the patience to look deeper. A little practice will soon reveal a trend: Some feelings evoke gratitude; others evoke contrition; still others open avenues for further reflection that may lead to life-changing decisions.

Looking to the Future with Hope

In this part of the prayer, I ask God to "help me do better tomorrow than I did today." But the grace I am seeking is not so narrow as a correction of the faults I've identified. I want to be a better disciple, to draw closer to Jesus, to look on all I see with love. The hope to which we are called is not merely forgiveness of our sins but a sharing in the life of Christ. No matter how long or short the future stretching before us, we live in hope.

The *examen* traditionally concludes with the Lord's Prayer.

Prayer Exercise: Who Do You Say That I Am?

In St. Luke's Gospel, the disciples tell Jesus some of the stories that are circulating about who Jesus might be. Some people think John the Baptist has come back to life; others associate Jesus with Elijah "or one of the prophets." Jesus asks, "But who do you say that I am?"

Relax and breathe deeply. Place yourself in the presence of God. Read Luke 9:18–20 slowly and attentively. Then, turn the question around; ask Jesus, *Who do you say that I am?*

Suggested Scripture Readings

The Ignatian approach to praying with Scripture is discussed in detail in the next chapter. The following are a few passages that may speak to someone exploring the question "Who am I now?"

- Luke 9:18–20
- Psalm 16
- Sirach 30:21–25

- Isaiah 6:1–8
- Jeremiah 29:11–14
- Matthew 6:25–34
- John 15:16–17

3

Decisions

To begin, ask yourself these questions:

What will I do when I retire?

Do I really need that big house?

We are constantly making choices, in matters serious and trivial, every day of our lives. A great deal of spiritual literature deals with moral choices that people face at any age, such as how to avoid sin and grow in grace. There has also been much emphasis traditionally on the kinds of decisions that are most often made in young adulthood: choosing a "state in life," such as marriage or priesthood.

The kinds of decisions that are faced by people in their sixties and older, such as those required by retirement, diminished capacity, and caregiving obligations, do not fit neatly into such traditional categories. Where, then, do we look for guidance? Newspapers, bookstores, and the Internet are full of do-it-yourself advice about saving for retirement and choosing areas of the country with the lowest cost of living or the best golf courses. But the God-centered person needs more substantive guidance on how to make later-life decisions in the context of seeing, loving, and following Jesus; on how to find God in all things.

Decisions particular to this stage of life can be divided into two major groups: "whether" decisions and "how" decisions. Retirement is often a "whether" decision; caregiving and diminished capacity are more likely to involve "how" decisions. Ignatian spirituality has guidance for both.

"Whether" Decisions

One of the biggest decisions for many people is whether and when to retire. The first consideration is often whether they will have enough to live on after retirement. The answer isn't as obvious as it may seem. "How much is enough?" depends on what assumptions we make about our standard of living after retirement, which can certainly affect the timing of retirement and, in the unforgiving economy of recent years, may lead to the decision to keep working indefinitely.

Another consideration is how long a person can expect to be physically and mentally able to continue doing the same job. The answer may be obvious for workers whose jobs are physically demanding, such as a nurse's aide who lifts heavy patients. It may be less so for a corporate executive who must be fully engaged in important meetings despite an exhausting travel schedule and debilitating jet lag. The nurse's aide may have an unequivocal signal in the form of chronic back pain, but for many people there is no bright line. In these circumstances, it is often easy to be in denial, refusing to admit that one's professional skills are not what they once were, or simply that one is too tired too much of the time to enjoy life.

A related question that often arises at or after retirement concerns downsizing. This topic is so important, in itself and in relation to Ignatius's advice, that it is considered separately in the next chapter.

Closely related to the decision to retire is the question of what to do in retirement. Generalized goals such as travel or spending time with family aren't really helpful unless they can be expressed concretely. Most people don't have the resources or inclination to spend all their time traveling; what, then, follows that trans-Pacific cruise or African safari? Does "spending time with family" mean doing more things with one's spouse, babysitting one's grandchildren, or sharing in caregiving responsibilities for another family member?

Should you have a definite plan or wait to see what occasions arise?

Following are topics to consider while making decisions about retirement.

Working. Some retired people opt for part-time jobs because they either need the money or want the structure and social interaction involved. The type of work available on this basis will vary greatly in different locations, but it is important to face the likelihood that the work will be less interesting or rewarding than one's former career.

Ministry of Service. Others may choose volunteer work. Many retired people welcome the opportunity to "give back" some of their talents and resources by helping others. There are innumerable opportunities to be of service in ways that fit one's interests. A recent Google search for "volunteer opportunities New York City" yielded more than seventeen million results. In most cities, the number and quality of choices is overwhelming: drive an ambulance; be a candy striper in a hospital; work with a neighborhood organization that plants flowers and tends to the upkeep of local parks; read for the blind; take the Eucharist to a hospital or nursing home; care for abandoned animals at a local shelter; or use your existing business or professional skills to help the poor. Some kinds of volunteer work require training, such as tutoring GED candidates, assisting immigrants applying for citizenship, or teaching religious education at a local parish. Other agencies just need more hands to stock food pantries, serve meals at homeless shelters, or answer phones.

Whatever one's interests, there is a tremendous advantage in service that includes a spiritual dimension. The Ignatian Volunteer Corps, which I mentioned in chapter 1, has members serving those in need through literally hundreds of different jobs: they hold regular meetings for prayer and faith sharing as well as lead retreats, provide spiritual direction and opportunities for spiritual reading and discussion. Other organizations at the parish, diocesan, or international level may provide a spiritual dimension in a variety of ways.

Finding the right fit involves some soul-searching. Why do I want to volunteer? Is it just to fill free time, or is there a cause I care about, a group of people I really want to help? Is there a religious dimension to the kind of work I am considering? Will this opportunity help me grow in my spiritual life, or will it divert my attention from it? Do I want to use the skills and knowledge from my former career, or would I be more comfortable with something entirely new? A lawyer acquaintance of mine retired from a demanding position as a partner of a major law firm and immediately went to work full-time for a not-for-profit legal organization. Many of my fellow Ignatian Volunteers choose to use their professional qualifications as nurses, social workers, and grant writers a few days a week in the service of the poor. I, on the other hand, told the Ignatian Volunteers coordinator that I was open to any kind of volunteer service *except* legal work—after all, I was retired from the legal profession!

Creativity. Others may discover that creativity can flower in later life. Michelangelo was eighty-eight when he sculpted his *Rondanini Pietà*, a much more profound treatment of the subject than the more famous version in St. Peter's Basilica, completed when the artist was twenty-four.[13] While few of us may have that kind of outsize talent, there are many ways of unlocking our inner creativity. A lawyer I knew wrote a book of wisdom for his grandchildren, for distribution to them after his death. A grandmother makes scrapbooks documenting her grandchildren's lives with photos, artwork, and other media. Painting seems to be a favorite late-life pursuit of retired politicians, including Winston Churchill, Dwight Eisenhower, and George W. Bush. I have had a lifelong interest in photography, but in recent years I have noticed a new way of seeing through the lens, "praying with the camera."

These and other means of expression offer opportunities for contemplation. We can all be open to new ideas, new graces, and a much deeper understanding of ourselves and our spiritual journey. God may be calling us to—who knows what?

In the face of any of these decisions, being well informed about the facts of a situation is a necessary starting point. The Internet has made essential information easier to find than was true even twenty years ago, but it still takes time and commitment to evaluate all of it. Then, the question is what criteria to apply in making a decision.

Ignatian Prayer: Decision Making

Ignatius devotes a great deal of space to what I have called "whether" questions. A substantial portion of his advice is devoted to what he calls "unchangeable elections," such as marriage or priesthood. This is unsurprising, considering the appropriateness of the Exercises, then and now, for young people making life decisions such as whether to enter the Society of Jesus. But for those of us trying to make shorter-term decisions appropriate to the situations in which we find ourselves, Ignatius also offers guidance on how to make what he calls a "changeable election," i.e., one that is not irrevocable. In this context, *election* means a choice between alternatives that are good, better, or neutral insofar as they relate to our living the Christian life. We are not talking about how to choose virtue over sin.[14]

It sometimes happens that, as Ignatius puts it, "God our Lord moves and attracts the will in such a way that a devout person, without doubting or being able to doubt, carries out what was proposed" (SpEx 175). The best choice appears with unmistakable clarity; all of one's impulses and feelings move toward it, and any alternatives seem dry or meaningless. Ignatius is not talking about mystical experience or a kind of grace given only to the saints. God, after all, can give grace to whomever he chooses, in whatever circumstance. When this kind of attraction occurs, it may be like being swept up in a powerful current or seeing a goal clearly illuminated. Whatever the metaphor, there is little room for doubt, and usually there is a feeling of peace.

Decisions such as when to retire or whether to sell a house may present themselves with that kind of certainty, but most people face competing considerations that need to be sorted out. In some circumstances there is a need to focus on conflicting feelings, which may be too strong for reasoned analysis. Ignatius's advice for those situations is discussed in the next chapter. Here we consider his advice on a rational way of proceeding.[15] His principles can be summarized in modern terms as follows:

1. Define the question.

2. Strive to be as detached as possible without assuming the result you prefer.

3. Ask God to move your will toward what pleases him and makes you a better Christian.

4. List and rationally consider the advantages and disadvantages.

5. Make a decision based on what seems most reasonable.

6. Bring the decision to prayer and ask God "to receive and confirm it" (SpEx 183).

Although prayer is expressly mentioned in only two of the six steps of the process, it is hardly excluded from the others. We can better understand the importance of prayer in the entire process by considering some of the kinds of decisions discussed in this chapter.

1. Define the question.

Consider a hypothetical couple living in a northern state, who take winter vacations in Florida or the Caribbean and have always dreamed of living all year in a warm climate. Newly retired, should they move? It may look like a yes-or-no question, but there are all kinds of subsidiary questions. In researching such things as the cost of living in the new community, the availability of public transportation and medical services, cultural resources, and opportunities to meet people, the couple may have to examine more closely what their priorities are. Are they willing to make substantial adjustments to their lifestyle? How will the move affect their relationships with children and grandchildren? What kind of relationship with their adult children do they want at this stage of their lives? In short, what is involved in such a move other than a change of climate?

While some of these issues need to be looked at more carefully at the fourth step, listing advantages and disadvantages, it should be clear that the process ought to begin with prayer for enlightenment in defining the decision to be made.

Define the question as concretely as possible. It is sometimes hard to formulate a yes-or-no question. There may be several alternatives, such as what I call "subsidiary questions" in the hypothetical example above. Richard Hauser, SJ, former chairman of the Department of Theology at Creighton University, suggests a procedure that may facilitate the process: List all the possibilities; next, identify the pros and cons of each; then, rank the alternatives in order of importance; and use the one at the top of the list as the defined question to use in the rest of the exercise.[16] I would add to this analysis that the process may illumine more than one important question, so that it may be profitable to repeat the exercise. However one approaches it, defining the question really is the most important part of the exercise, and it deserves a substantial commitment of time and reflection.

2. Strive for detachment.

This may be the most difficult step for many people. The kinds of decisions we face in later life can be highly emotional: retirement from work with which our identity may be bound up, leaving a home with a lifetime of memories for a situation that may involve dependence. Ignatius's advice is to see oneself as "the pointer of a balance," that is, "not more inclined or emotionally disposed toward" one choice or the other.[17] That may seem an almost unattainable goal in an emotionally charged situation. How can I possibly feel the same way about retiring as about working? About leaving my home as staying in it? The answer, which is not at all obvious, is to try as much as possible to set the feelings aside and examine the matter rationally. One way of testing our ability to do this is to apply what lawyers call the "reasonable person standard": How would an ordinary, reasonable person assess the situation? Or, in Ignatius's language, where would such a person place the pointer of the balance?

The prayer at step 2, then, should be for the grace to set aside feelings and calmly consider the reasons that should inform the choice.

3. Ask God to move your will.

Perhaps there are strong emotional pulls in both directions. You may really want to keep working at a job you love, but you have always looked forward to a time when your days were not governed by clocks and deadlines. Your spouse may want to keep working longer or may want to retire sooner. Your work may have become a physical and emotional burden that you no longer feel equal to, but you fear financial insecurity. You may realize that you are no longer up to the demands of your job, but you still want to continue.

In these and many similar situations, it may be difficult to proceed to a rational analysis of the consequences. The emotional force may simply be too strong—if we are relying solely on our own power. This is a point at which we really need to recognize and acknowledge our dependence on God. The prayer at step 3, then, should be for God to move your will toward the choice that is consonant with your life's journey as a Christian in an ever-growing relationship with the Creator. God indeed can move the will, sometimes toward choices we might never have imagined.

4. Assess advantages and disadvantages of each alternative.

Having aimed for detachment and then asked God to move the will, we are in the right frame of mind to identify and weigh the advantages and disadvantages of each alternative. This is a deliberative process that may require substantial time. The ramifications of major decisions can rarely be articulated in fifteen minutes or listed on a single page. A person thinking of selling a house, for example, would need to estimate how much might be realized from the sale and the affordability of alternative living arrangements. This in turn would require accurate information about, among other things, the real-estate market in the area; the condition of the property; whether the sale would result in a profit; and how predictable the cost of realistic alternative living arrangements would be. A move to a warmer climate might entail less frequent contact with children and grandchildren, or it might afford the opportunity to learn a new skill or to do a new kind of volunteer work.

An important caution at this stage is to consider the quality, not merely the quantity, of the pros and cons. There may be only one consideration on the "pro" side, but it may outweigh six or seven trivial "cons"—or vice versa.

5. Make a decision based on what seems most reasonable.

Notice that this step assumes both a sincere effort at detachment in step 2 and a thorough and careful analysis in step 4. The "reasonable person standard" may be helpful here. But if it seems particularly difficult to make a choice, it might be profitable to review the previous steps, if time permits. Otherwise, it is important to recognize that 100 percent certainty is rare in life. The missing part is trust in God.

6. Offer the decision to God in prayer.

Asking God to "receive and confirm" the decision should flow naturally from what has gone before.[18] How do we know that God has confirmed the decision? Many commentators on Ignatian spirituality suggest that we may find new reasons to support the decision, feel more emotionally drawn to it, or experience a growing feeling of certainty and a new sense of peace. This final step, which may take some time, is another way of asking God for the grace to live the decision and to find God in all things.

"How" Decisions

Some of the decisions that arise in the later stages of life do not fit neatly into either-or categories but are more open-ended. Finding out what the options are may not be easy. Some examples are

- how to treat an illness, an issue that is not always straightforward, as the experience of Joseph in the preceding chapter illustrates;
- how to care for an invalid spouse or parent, which includes a whole panoply of issues that may involve whether and where to find help, either from family members or paid professionals; how to safeguard one's own health; whether assisted living, a nursing home, or hospice care is appropriate, and if so, where, and how to pay for it; and not least, how to give emotional support to the patient;
- how to respond to diminished capacity, such as when to stop driving or living alone;
- how to respond to children who insist on "helping"—or telling you what to do;
- how to spend one's "free" time; and
- how to approach one's spiritual journey as its length diminishes.

While the Spiritual Exercises do not specifically address any of these modern issues, they do contain wisdom that is as applicable in our times as in any other.

After discussing the process of choosing a "state of life," Ignatius goes on to counsel that we should "think about how we ought to dispose ourselves to come to perfection in whatever state of life God our Lord may grant us to elect."[19] The formality of the language, even in modern translation, is a bit off-putting. A contemporary formulation for older adults might be, "How can I grow in grace, where I am, here and now?"

For Ignatius, the starting point is always to focus on Jesus, who took on our humanity so that we might learn how to be fully human. In one well-known example, Ignatius advises that when eating and drinking, one should try to imagine how Jesus conducted himself at table and then "try to imitate him."[20] This should not be reduced to "What would Jesus do?" (often asked as a preface to a predetermined answer). Rather, it should be a reminder to reflect on Jesus as our model in all things.

In the full Exercises, Ignatius introduces the principles of decision making at a point when the retreatant is asked to meditate on the life and ministry of Jesus from the time of his baptism in the Jordan to his arrival in Jerusalem on Palm Sunday. He thus reminds us at the outset that the answers to questions about how to live begin and end with Jesus.

One way to model ourselves after Jesus is by praying with Scripture.

Ignatian Prayer: Praying with Scripture

While Scripture study is always valuable, it is not the same as praying with Scripture. Study emphasizes intellectual knowledge—for example, about the authorship of various books of the Bible, their cultural context, or the major theories of interpretation. This kind of knowledge can inform our prayer, but it isn't prayer. Praying with Scripture sees the Bible as the living word, a channel for a closer relationship with God. The two principal ways of praying with Scripture in the Ignatian tradition are *lectio divina* (usually translated as "holy reading") and imaginative prayer. Some people prefer one over the other, but they are not mutually exclusive.

In *lectio divina*, the emphasis is on the *words* of Scripture. The very title—"reading"—makes this clear. We read a passage slowly and attentively, several times over. We look for a word or phrase that stands out, and we savor it, turning it over in our minds, taking it into our hearts. We can ask ourselves, *Why does this word or phrase resonate with me here and now?* The language may illuminate a recent gift of grace, a weakness, or a pressing problem. *What is God saying to me?* We may want to simply rest awhile in our awareness of the presence of God in the living word. Then we may ask, *What do I want to say to God?*

Whatever insights have come to us we can bring to God in words of thanksgiving, repentance, or earnest supplication.

In imaginative prayer, the emphasis is on *images*. We try to visualize the situation as though we ourselves were there. We focus first on the details of the scene, perhaps searching for details omitted from a succinct Gospel passage. For example, Ignatius imagined Mary on the road to Bethlehem "seated on a burro; and with her were Joseph and a servant girl, leading an ox."[21] Whatever our initial image of the scene, we should try to experience it by imagining the sights, sounds, smells, tastes, and textures.

What do the people in the episode look like? Are they young or old? Families with children? Are they well-dressed or in rags? Watch.

What are they saying? Are they shouting or whispering, or are they silent, listening to Jesus? What other sounds can I hear: horses, birds, children shouting, someone playing a flute, goats with bells around their necks? Listen.

What can I smell: fresh-caught fish? The wind off the Sea of Galilee? Breathe.

Can I taste the wine at the dinner of Simon the Pharisee? At the Last Supper? Savor.

Is Jesus touching a leper, a blind man, a woman washing his feet with precious ointment? Is Jesus touching me? What does his touch feel like? Yield.

From the sense impressions, it is an easy step to the feelings evoked by the scene. With whom do I identify: the forgiven sinner, the woman at the well, a skeptical onlooker in the crowd? How do I feel about what I have seen and heard? How do I feel about Jesus? What is Jesus saying to me? Listen. What do I want to say to Jesus? Speak to him.

People new to imaginative prayer sometimes object that they don't know enough about daily life in ancient times to place themselves in the scene. For example, they can't imagine how the crowds who followed Jesus would have been dressed, what Matthew's tax station looked like, or what kind of food Martha was preparing when she complained to Jesus that she needed her sister's help. There are several answers to this objection.

First, the emphasis is on our own feelings. If I identify with Martha, or for that matter with her sister, Mary, do I really need detailed cinematography? How does it feel to be doing all the work while the person who should be helping is sitting at Jesus' feet? How does it feel to experience the grace of Jesus' presence, only to be called away by a nagging sister? Can I tell Jesus how I feel? What is his response? Listen.

For those who feel better able to enter the prayer with the help of greater detail, it isn't necessary to go back to school. Fiction, films, and art provide many resources.

Good historical fiction often presents a more vivid picture of daily life in ancient times than biblical commentary or history. Films can be even more evocative. There are some suggestions in the Ignatian Resources, but most readers will be able to find on their own the works that speak to them.

For those who think more visually than verbally, religious art can be evocative. In the West, the art of the Middle Ages focused almost exclusively on biblical subjects, and the Renaissance produced some of the greatest religious art of all time. In the Eastern churches, praying with icons is an ancient tradition. Henri J. M. Nouwen spent several days sitting in front of Rembrandt's *The Return of the Prodigal Son* in The Hermitage, St. Petersburg. The painting, like much of Rembrandt's mature work, focuses on the character of each of the principals: the father and his two sons. Nouwen lingered long and thoughtfully over the smallest details, such as the position of the father's hands and the subtleties of light and shadow. As he went deeper into the images, he could experience the father's love and the conflicting emotions of each of the sons. The book that resulted from this experience,

The Return of the Prodigal Son, is a primer on the richness of imaginative prayer.

It isn't necessary to go to St. Petersburg or Rome or even to the nearest museum (although there are rich resources in most major cities). Many museums have made large parts of their collections available online, and these databases are only likely to grow. Some religious art is actually easier to appreciate in a good-quality reproduction than on-site. The ceiling of the Sistine Chapel in the Vatican comes immediately to mind, especially for any of us with limited range of motion in our aging necks.[22]

Finally, one of the most noticeable things about religious art is how often the artist has used the landscapes and costumes of his own time. Medieval artists knew little or nothing about Judea in the time of Jesus, so they painted landscapes with medieval towers and showed women wearing the elaborate headdresses common in Europe at that time. If we imagine Peter's mother-in-law getting up to prepare a meal for Jesus after he has cured her, there is nothing wrong with picturing her in our own kitchen. Perhaps we can use our modern appliances to offer hospitality to someone who has just done us a great favor? Or to someone who can offer us nothing but has needs that we can meet? In meditating on the arraignment of Jesus before Pilate (Luke 23:1–5), I have imagined what the scene might have been like in the Magistrate Judges Courtroom at the old federal courthouse in Foley Square. Pilate's attempt to pass the buck to Herod was not very different from transferring a prisoner from federal to state custody—which in New York City is directly across the street. The federal marshals making the transfer would have to take a circuitous route to avoid the protesting crowds on the steps. I wonder how the Roman soldiers managed transporting Jesus to Herod's court?

Imaginative prayer is particularly appropriate for praying with passages that describe an event in the life or ministry of Jesus, such as the visit of the Magi, the multiplication of loaves and fishes, or the cure of a blind man. *Lectio divina*, on the other hand, is well suited to more abstract passages without visual imagery, such as St. Paul's meditation on love, or Jesus' promise of the coming of the Holy Spirit, in the Last Discourse. There is no bright line dividing the two types of prayer, and both can help us to know, love, and imitate Jesus.

Prayer Exercise: Imagining the Life of Christ

Do an online search for "Nativity Scene Old Masters" and click on "Images." Choose one that appeals to you and that you can view full screen.[23]

Look first at the light in the picture: Where is it coming from? Who is illuminated? Are there areas of darkness as well? Who or what is in the dark space? Where are you—in the light or in the dark?

Look closely at each figure in the picture, one at a time. Don't rush. You may want to start with some of the figures on the outer fringes of the picture, such as shepherds. Notice the expression on each of their faces: Which of them is feeling awe? Surprise? Confusion? Curiosity? Joy? Which ones are trying to get closer? Which are hanging back? Can you identify with one of these shepherds? Why are you there? What do you see? How do you feel about it?

Look at Mary. Does she look like a woman who has just given birth, or has the artist idealized her? Imagine how she might have looked an hour or two earlier. Is she still in pain from the birth? What is the expression on her face now? How does she feel about the sudden visit of the shepherds? Have they told her what they heard and saw in the fields? And, if so, is she surprised? Is there something you want to ask her?

Is Joseph in the picture? How old is he? Is he (as he is often depicted in art) worshipping the baby Jesus? What emotions do his face and body language suggest? Can you identify with Joseph? How would you feel about caring for a child born in a stable when you are far from home? What are you going to say to all these shepherds?

Look at the baby Jesus. Does he look like a real newborn baby? Do you want to pick him up and hold him? Ask Mary's permission to pick him up. What will you say to him?

The variations are infinite—and, of course, you don't have to choose the Nativity.

Suggested Scripture Readings

The difficulty with any selective list is that it leaves out more than it includes. The Gospel of the day is often a good place to begin. Among many other sources, the day's readings can be found on the Web site of the U.S. Conference of Catholic Bishops, http://www.usccb.org/bible/readings. The following passages deal with situations and teachings that may resonate with older adults.

For Imaginative Prayer

- Luke 2:22–38 (Simeon and Anna)
- Luke 7:11–17 (Raising of the Widow's Son)
- Luke 10:38–42 (Martha and Mary)
- Luke 15:11–32 (The Prodigal Son)
- Luke 18:18–23 ("What must I do to inherit eternal life?")

- Luke 21:1–4 (The Widow's Mite)
- John 4:1–29 (The Woman at the Well)

For *Lectio Divina*

- Luke 6:20–26 (Sermon on the Plain)
- Luke 18:18–23 ("What must I do to inherit eternal life?")
- Luke 21:1–4 (The Widow's Mite)
- John 1:1–5 or 1:1–14 ("In the beginning was the Word.")
- John 14:1–7, 25–28; 15:1–5, 11–17 (Last Discourse)
- 1 Corinthians 12:4–11 (Different Gifts)
- 1 Corinthians 13:1–13 ("Love never fails.")
- 2 Corinthians 7–10 (Strength in Weakness)

4

Downsizing

To begin, ask yourself these questions:

What do I really need?

What do I most fear?

Many older adults confront questions relating to scaling down their lifestyle: moving to a smaller home, giving up a car, letting go of material things. The aging also face physical and mental losses that involve a different kind of downsizing—or, more accurately, a kind of poverty that has nothing to do with wealth or possessions. Accepting help—let alone asking for it!—may also present special challenges. Fear of the unknown or of loss and diminishment may color any of these issues.

Ignatius's rules for decision making and his advice about imitating Jesus are certainly helpful in all these situations.

But decisions of these kinds, more than most others, require us to look deeply into who we are and what we value. Ignatius's analytical approach to decision making, discussed in the preceding chapter, may be less useful. We may instead need to discover how God speaks to us through our feelings. We need, in short, a discerning heart.

How Much Is Enough?

Many older adults find that they no longer need, or have the energy to maintain, a large house. Whether to move from a longtime home is often a radically life-changing decision and a wrenching emotional one. How to carry out such a decision may be even more complicated. There are many variations.

Some have the option of moving in with their adult children. Matilda's story, in chapter 2, is a cautionary tale about the kinds of pitfalls such a decision may involve. Others may wish to establish their own households in the cities or towns where their children live. This, too, has perils. I once worked with a lawyer who decided to move to another state after retirement because his only son was living there with his family. My colleague and his wife returned to New York after a year because they knew no one except their son's family and missed the active, connected life they had enjoyed in their former community. For many people, there are underlying (and often overlooked) questions relating to the kind of relationship they want to have with their adult children at this stage of life. Preserving independence as long as possible is an objective frequently mentioned when people are surveyed about their goals and concerns. Will that objective be furthered or hampered by living with or near one's children? Would assisted living be a better or worse option?

Housing is only one area of potential downsizing. Expenses that were necessary during full-time employment may now be luxuries. One car can do the former work of two; reduced income or diminished capacity may mean no car at all.

As the population ages, practical questions such as these have begun to be analyzed in publications addressed to the general reader. The investment firm Merrill Lynch had a section on its Web site not long ago dealing exclusively with the financial advantages of downsizing. But downsizing is not a mere financial transaction. Whether the changes are necessary or merely practical, they inevitably involve an examination of core values. What really matters at this stage of life, at this stage of the spiritual journey?

Not all of us are called to lives of evangelical poverty, even in old age. Many retired people have an IRA or a 401(k) plan that may or may not be sufficient. Some have substantial property, others barely enough to live on. Most of us need to make prudent provision so that we do not outlive our money. Some of us may also ask: How much of our money should outlive us? There is no one-size-fits-all approach. The answers will be different for a single person with no family and a couple with children and grandchildren, but all should ask the question: How much is enough?

Ignatius's advice on property is a useful starting point. He teaches that we should "desire to keep it or dispose of it solely according to what God our Lord will move [our] will to choose" and should not "desire or feel . . . strongly attached to have wealth rather than poverty, or honor rather than dishonor, or a long life rather than a short one." With this in mind, Ignatius counsels very specific attention to such matters as how large a household to maintain and how much to spend on one's lifestyle.[24]

For many Americans, Ignatius's admonition not to prefer wealth over poverty can be a stumbling block. Those of us who have worked hard all our lives feel a sense of entitlement to the fruits of our labor. "I've earned it" is not a Christian attitude; it is a cultural assumption and one that calls for honest prayer and prudent discernment.

We may not all have the grace to embrace the Ignatian ideal of a genuine preference for poverty, but we may still find greater clarity in distinguishing what we really need for a well-balanced life. For me, it meant the painful decision to give up my car: a necessity when I was working, a luxury in New York City in retirement. For others, it might mean moving from a house to an apartment, cutting down on spending, making gifts to children or grandchildren, or letting go of possessions that are no longer needed. A neighbor of mine, then in her eighties, told me proudly that she and her husband were "de-accessioning" the artworks acquired over a lifetime of collecting, because she knew her children had no interest in inheriting them.

No matter how modest our circumstances, Ignatius reminds us of the need to provide "for the poor and other good works." Retirees on limited incomes may be able to make only small financial contributions, but for many of us the opportunity to give our time and talents in service can be a special grace. The opportunity to do volunteer work is for many people a new kind of vocation. Downsizing can thus help us focus on social justice, not only in what we give to the poor but also in what we might be called to do.

A Different Kind of Poverty

In his post-resurrection appearance to the disciples at the Sea of Tiberias, Jesus says to Peter:

> Amen, amen, I say to you, when you were younger, you
> used to dress yourself and go where you wanted; but
> when you grow old, you will stretch out your hands, and
> someone else will dress you and lead you where you do
> not want to go. (John 21:18)

Although Jesus "said this signifying by what kind of death
[Peter] would glorify God" (John 21:19), for many aging
people it is a promise of diminished capacity and loss of independence. Those changes may be seen as a kind of poverty
unrelated to money or property.

Sooner or later, our bodies begin to fail us. We need bifo-
cals, periodontal surgery, cataract surgery, knee replacements,
hearing aids. Starting in middle age, these common medical interventions seem almost like rites of passage. They also
remind us that many of our body parts are not well adapted
to the long life spans most of us enjoy in the twenty-first century. As we gradually begin to admit that we can no longer
call ourselves middle-aged, many of us experience losses in
hearing, vision, or mobility that medical science can do little
or nothing to arrest.

Then there is fear. The biggest fear for many older adults is
the loss of mental faculties: loss of memory, difficulty express-
ing oneself, and worst of all, dementia. We often hear people
say, "I don't want to be a burden," when what they mean is,

"I am terrified of not knowing who I am or what is happening to me." The late Thomas Clarke, SJ, has called this "our special brand of poverty."

Arthritis makes it difficult for me to climb stairs or get up from very low seats; things I can no longer do include riding the New York City subway, sitting in a theater balcony, and using a bathtub rather than a shower. I know people in my age group who have experienced profound hearing loss or debilitating pain that makes social life impossible. These losses are indeed a special kind of poverty—different in kind from the experiences of the materially poor, yet poverty nonetheless. It is also a particularly lonely kind of poverty: Can younger, healthier people even imagine the fear of losing one's independence, one's memory, one's identity?

Grace was a religious sister who, in her seventies, began to have increasing difficulty finding the right word. Before she was diagnosed, she realized that she was in the early stages of Alzheimer's disease. Resisting the fear that inevitably accompanies such knowledge, she embraced her diminishing capacity as a new call to ministry. She saw herself in solidarity with others who were losing their cognitive abilities and sense of self, and she committed to pray for them as long as she was able. The last time I saw her, before she moved to her community's facility for the elderly and infirm, her ability to express herself verbally had noticeably deteriorated, but she radiated peace and happiness.

Mary was a single woman who, also in her seventies, began experiencing memory loss, which was later followed by significant vocabulary loss. She retired from full-time work and began bit by bit to withdraw from activities she had always enjoyed, including going to the opera and serving as a Eucharistic minister. Her only family consisted of siblings in another state. For a long time she resisted their efforts to persuade her to move from her walk-up apartment to assisted living. She knew that once she gave up her independence, she would never regain it. Always deeply religious, she did not cease praying even as she lacked the words. I had not heard from her in a while, because talking on the phone was a challenge for her. Then, one day she called to tell me of her move to a beautiful one-bedroom apartment in an assisted-living facility. She was not far from two of her sisters and was overjoyed that she was allowed to keep her cat. How her sisters finally overcame her resistance I don't know. What was clear was that, even as Mary's ability to describe her feelings diminished, she had found the grace in this unlooked-for stage of life.

Letting go of mobility, of hearing, of independence, may be much more difficult than letting go of material things, especially since we do not choose these physical losses. Here, too, one size does not fit all. Old-fashioned advice like "offer it up" or "live in the present moment" may make the matter worse. But this may be a time in our lives when we can acknowledge our total dependence on God.

On a recent Holy Thursday, I was struck by how the Gospel of Jesus washing the feet of the disciples (John 13:1–15) leads to this insight. I tried to imagine myself as one of the disciples, as Jesus approached to wash my feet. My first reaction was a lot like Peter's: *No, Lord, don't wash my feet; don't touch me; I am a sinner; my little heart cannot contain such an enormous act of love.* I managed to overcome that feeling, as Peter had. Then my imagination took me to the possibility of a time in the future when I might have to depend on others, not only to wash my feet and "my head and hands as well" but also to help me with many simple everyday tasks. Will I be able to see Christ in the caregivers?

Ignatius prescribes a meditation on St. Matthew's version of the Beatitudes during the Second Week of the Spiritual Exercises. In the translation commonly used in the United States, the opening verse is "Blessed are the poor in spirit, for theirs is the kingdom of heaven" (Matthew 5:3). The Jerusalem Bible, which is popular in countries that use British English, instead begins "How happy are the poor in spirit" and uses "happy" instead of "blessed" throughout the Beatitudes.[25] Are we really supposed to be *happy* about being materially poor, or about the poverty that comes from physical or mental diminishment? How is any of this a blessing? Where is the grace in all this?[26]

Again, I keep coming back to our dependence on God. That is in fact what "the poor in spirit" is usually understood to mean: those who are aware of their total dependence on God. Thus, the promise of the "kingdom of heaven" is not a mere reference to some future eternal reward. Rather, Jesus is saying that the awareness of our dependence on God is itself a gift. I have no doubt that was how Sister Grace came to embrace what she saw as a new kind of vocation.

Interestingly, Ignatius does not prescribe Luke's version of the Beatitudes (6:20–26), which begins "Blessed [happy] are you who are poor." This version may speak more directly to those of us experiencing increasing impoverishment, material or physical. Either way, we should allow ourselves to be led to a more profound understanding that *all is gift*: every beat of our heart, every breath we take, and every way we are permitted to enjoy life and praise God for as long as God wills. As long as we are alive, there is something to be thankful for.

This may sound like an oversimplification, especially for people who are experiencing severe pain or crippling disability. I cannot speak from personal experience about such extreme situations, but I do take comfort in the well-worn principle that we are given the grace that is appropriate to the situation we are in. When we are healthy, we may not be able to imagine how we would cope with a terminal illness. Nor should we. We don't need that grace now. When the time comes, so will the grace, provided we are open to receiving it.

God does not force us to accept grace; we can always choose to refuse it. To perceive what our choices are, we need to pay attention. Elijah did not find God in the storm or the earthquake or the fire but in "a tiny whispering sound" (1 Kings 19:11–13). The skills we need to hear what God is whispering to us are what Ignatius called discernment of spirits.

Ignatian Prayer: Discernment of Spirits

Discernment of spirits is not really a form of prayer. Rather, it is a type of awareness that can enrich and deepen our prayer as we learn to distinguish *what draws us closer to God and what draws us away.*

To do this, we prayerfully examine our feelings, what Ignatius called the "motions" of the heart. I prefer Richard Hauser's phrase *fluctuations of the heart,* which better conveys both the subtlety and the fleeting nature of the thoughts, feelings, and impulses that often underlie our actions.[27] Those facing downsizing or the poverty that comes with diminishment and loss may find this a particularly appropriate time to ask God for the grace of a discerning heart.

In his autobiography, Ignatius described his first experience of what he later came to call discernment of spirits.[28] During his long recovery from a wound sustained in battle and a series of ghastly sixteenth-century surgeries, he had little to read and a great deal of time to let his thoughts run in all directions. He indulged in elaborate fantasies about feats he might accomplish when restored to health and, in particular, how they might favorably impress a certain noble lady. His reading of the lives of Christ and the saints—the only books available to him—also generated fantasies. He imagined himself imitating St. Dominic and St. Francis and was attracted to extreme self-denial. He dwelt at length on both kinds of fantasies and eventually noticed an important difference. The worldly thoughts, while pleasurable, "left him dry and dissatisfied."[29] The thoughts of imitating the saints had a strikingly different effect: "not only was he consoled when he had these thoughts, but even after putting them aside he remained satisfied and joyful."[30] Gradually he began to reflect on the differences and "came to recognize the difference between the spirits that were stirring, one from the devil, the other from God."[31]

The modern reader may have more difficulty than Ignatius did in personifying the good and evil impulses as God and the devil, or as good and evil spirits. Scholars of Ignatian spirituality in our own time have understood these terms more broadly. Thus, "evil spirits" can mean any internal or external influence that turns us away from God, such as our tendencies toward egotism or the values of the secular world around us. "Good spirits" are all the opposites. It is in that comprehensive sense that I will use these terms.[32]

The fluctuations of the heart caused by the different spirits lead to conditions of *spiritual consolation* and *spiritual desolation*. Understanding these feelings and learning how to respond to them are the characteristics of a discerning heart.

The crux of spiritual desolation is the feeling of *separation from God*. In Ignatius's words, "it is characteristic of the evil spirit to cause gnawing anxiety, to sadden, and to set up obstacles" to spiritual progress.[33] In the worst-case scenario, these impulses "move one toward lack of faith and leave one without hope and without love. One is completely listless, tepid, and unhappy, and feels separated from our Creator and Lord."

Spiritual desolation is not the same as depression, although the two may coincide. Clinical depression involves deep feelings of sadness and hopelessness and increasing lack of interest in people and in formerly pleasurable activities. These feelings are often accompanied by physical symptoms such as loss of energy and changes in sleep patterns or appetite. A person who experiences these feelings over a substantial period should seek therapy. While sadness and negative feelings may also be present in spiritual desolation, the key indicator here is *disinclination to prayer*.[34]

One of the most striking examples of spiritual desolation was that experienced by St. Thérèse of Lisieux near the end of her life. In her autobiography, she describes her soul as in "pitch-black darkness" that lasted for many months. Trying to find consolation in thoughts of eternal life, she instead saw only "a still darker night, the night of annihilation!" She had not even "the consolation of faith." At this point in her narrative, she expresses the fear that to say any more about this lack of faith and hope might amount to "blasphemy."[35] One modern biographer has gone so far as to assert that "by the mid-winter of 1897 [a few months before her death], she had passed beyond all likely or even possible retrieval of faith and hope in a celestial life."[36] Yet she persisted in love, and even in her "night of [the] soul," she could write: "For me, prayer is an upward leap of the heart, an untroubled glance towards heaven, a cry of gratitude and love which I utter from the depths of sorrow as well as from the heights of joy."[37]

There is no evidence that Thérèse had ever read Ignatius. She nevertheless seems a perfect example of how a soul in utter hopelessness can persevere in prayer, knowing at some level of her being that God's grace is always sufficient, no matter how deep the darkness.

Spiritual consolation, on the other hand, includes "every increase in hope, faith, and charity, and every interior joy which calls and attracts one toward heavenly things and to the salvation of one's soul, by bringing it tranquility and peace in its Creator and Lord." It is a gift of God that Ignatius cautions us to receive with humility and use as a means to "store up new strength" against times of desolation.[38]

Spiritual consolation is not the same thing as feeling good. It can be given during times of sadness. I had such an experience during my Nineteenth Annotation retreat. The Third Week of the Exercises is devoted to meditating on the Passion and death of Jesus. It happened that I reached this point just before Easter. At the beginning of Holy Week, my father entered the hospital for a minor procedure and was found to have lung cancer requiring immediate surgery. On the train from New York to Hartford early on the morning of Good

Friday, full of sadness and worry, I was reading the Passion narratives and trying to place myself among the sorrowful women at the foot of the Cross. Suddenly I realized that *they didn't know how the story ended.* How total their desolation must have been without knowledge of the Resurrection! It was an extraordinary experience of entering the minds and hearts, and sharing the experience of, the companions of Jesus. At the same time, it was an experience of hope, because *we do know how the story ended.* This spiritual consolation strengthened and empowered me for the difficult days ahead. It was not a happy time, but it was a time of grace.

Discernment about Downsizing

What, then, has all this to do with making decisions, especially the ones faced by the aging? Decisions about downsizing may involve conflicting emotions, often magnified by family dynamics. Try as we might, we do not experience the tranquility necessary to make a rational decision according to the analytical method discussed in the preceding chapter. Instead of trying to ignore these powerful emotions, we look deeply within them to find "sufficient clarity and knowledge" on which to base a decision.[39] To avoid rash decisions or self-deception, we need to distinguish the fluctuations of the heart that come from the evil spirit and those that come from God.

Ignatius uses three metaphors to illustrate the way the evil spirit works to draw the soul away from God.[40] The first may be interpreted as that of a "spoiled child." This evil spirit focuses our attention on every trivial detail in a situation that does not meet our expectations, so that we do not look for the grace in the situation. I once met this devil on a retreat: The bed was uncomfortable; the room was cold; the shower malfunctioned; and breakfast was inadequate. I was so focused on these annoyances that I could not pray—until I recognized what was happening: The evil spirit certainly did not want me to pray! It is not hard to imagine how the same process might play out in the case of, for example, a newly retired person who finds many things to complain about in his or her new situation. The more one focuses on the disappointments and inconveniences, the harder it is to open up to the graces of the new environment.

The second metaphor is that of a "false lover" who draws us away from God through secrecy. If there is a trivial matter that one does not want to mention in confession because it is not seriously sinful, the evil spirit may be beckoning a person down a slippery slope, from the insignificant to the deadly. At a subtler level, when deciding what to discuss with a spiritual director, the uncomfortable topic that one would prefer to leave out is probably the one most deserving of attention. Subtler still is the impulse to avoid certain topics in prayer. It is easy enough to skip over something like anger or resentment, perhaps with an excuse such as lack of time or the rationalization that other topics are more important. A key part of the *examen* is focusing on what needs improvement in our spiritual journey, and this inevitably requires addressing our most intractable faults and those we have trouble acknowledging.

In my own prayer, I have often returned to a person I trusted who hurt me deeply and whom I had great difficulty forgiving. In the immediate wake of the event, I brought to prayer my resentment and anger, which dominated my daily *examen* to the point of giving very short shrift to everything else that mattered during the day. I reacted by trying to suppress all thoughts of the episode, to put them completely out of my mind. But, of course, the feelings were still there, festering beneath the surface. For a long time, I prayed for the grace to forgive the person who hurt me instead of trying to forget what happened. Eventually, I was able to move away from reexperiencing the resentment and the hurt, but I learned from this experience that recognizing the obligation to forgive is not the same as forgiveness from the heart.

For the aging, there are often painful situations calling for forgiveness, sometimes arising out of long-standing family conflicts and enduring hurts. It is all too easy to avoid thinking of these things. Allowing repressed feelings to surface brings to light what the evil spirit would prefer to keep in darkness. Some people have difficulty with the idea of bringing anger to prayer; it goes against a lot of what we were taught as children about how we "should" pray. But recognizing a bad feeling is not the same as accepting it, much less acting on it. The more we understand our negative impulses, the more we can ask for, and accept, the grace to act against them.

Another way the evil spirit may use the temptation to secrecy is to turn us away from help we may need. Refusing offers of help from family members or neighbors may be rationalized as a desire for privacy, but it could mean that a person is in denial. My mother began to lose her hearing when she was in her sixties, but when she died at age ninety-one, she was still insisting that she "wasn't ready" for a hearing aid. Something as simple as repeatedly postponing visits to the doctor or as dangerous as concealing the lack of food on hand may proceed from this kind of negative thinking.

The third metaphor Ignatius uses is that of a military commander who attacks us at our weakest point. In the face of impoverishment, material or otherwise, people are often beset by fear. Without minimizing the very real basis for some of these fears, they can certainly provide the kind of vulnerability suggested by Ignatius. In short, the evil spirit magnifies every what-if in an effort to make the fear controlling. Recognizing this dynamic can open us to respond with trust.

Ignatius also cautions that the evil angel sometimes "takes on the appearance of an angel of light."[41] One of the forms this took in his own life was the experience of vivid spiritual insights while he was studying. Aware of the importance of study in the life to which he felt called, he gradually came to realize that the spiritual insights drawing him away from study were in fact temptations. On a much more mundane level, while writing this book, I have often had my best ideas during prayer time.

Spiritual desolation can occur at any age or in any circumstances, but we should not be surprised if it occurs when life-changing decisions are in prospect. Ignatius cautions strongly against making significant changes during a time of spiritual desolation. As the "counterattack" to this condition, he instead urges increased prayer and meditation, patience, and, above all, confidence that the desolation will pass and God's grace will be sufficient. The guidance of a spiritual director, discussed below, can be especially helpful in times of spiritual desolation.[42]

The appropriate response to spiritual consolation, on the other hand, is first and foremost to give thanks to God for this gift of grace. For many people, aging brings greater interest in an inner journey. That does not mean merely more prayer or less fear of death but a deeper appreciation that all is gift, and a growing ability to find God in all things.

Discernment in Times of Involuntary Poverty

Discernment of spirits, then, is a means to wise and God-centered decision making. But the impoverishment experienced by many of the aging is involuntary. We do not decide to lose our hearing or to suffer a debilitating disease. What do good and evil spirits have to do with how we live now?

No matter how restricted our circumstances, we still make choices. We did not choose the pain, but we can choose how we respond to it. Easier said than done? Yes, of course. But that is precisely why it matters to understand how God is speaking to us through our feelings. As we advance in discernment, recognizing the fluctuations of the heart as they occur, we can come to a deeper understanding that our relationship with God is the purpose of our lives.

As we ask for the grace of a discerning heart, there is great practical help in both keeping a spiritual journal and meeting regularly with a spiritual director.

Keeping a Spiritual Journal

A spiritual journal is a regular record of spiritual experiences, insights, consolations, and desolations. They are best written down as soon as they occur, before memory has faded and their significance is lost. The end of the *examen* can be an excellent time. Some people write long, detailed accounts; others prefer key words or phrases, or even diagrams or drawings. A quotation from a verse of Scripture that stands out on a particular day may be all that is needed to bring the experience to mind. At other times, a detailed description of the experience may help you understand it more fully.

The main reason for keeping a regular spiritual journal is to observe the patterns in one's spiritual life over time. That may be particularly true of the pros and cons of a proposed decision as they unfold. As suggested earlier, it is also important to record experiences of spiritual consolation, to return to them in times of desolation or dryness. Combining journaling with spiritual direction can be especially enriching.

Spiritual Direction

A spiritual director is a person trained to help another develop a closer relationship to God. This ministry includes priests, religious, and laypeople. *Spiritual direction* is something of a misnomer, because the relationship rarely involves giving directions or instructions. It might be more accurately described as spiritual companionship. The director may also be considered a facilitator or a mentor who helps the directee to both a deeper appreciation of God's presence and a more loving response, always in the context of the presence of the Holy Spirit. The task of a spiritual director has been variously described as listening attentively, sympathetically, or empathetically. I prefer to call it "listening with the heart."[43]

Spiritual direction thus differs significantly from counseling. The counselor is expected to give practical advice, to help "fix" problems. The spiritual director's role, in contrast, is to evoke the directee's spiritual experience. The goal is not to tell the directee what to do but to help the directee to greater awareness of God and his or her own responses to that awareness. For me as a new director, this has been a challenge: When one of my directees is in a dark place, my first inclination is to talk about how God loves her unconditionally and about all the graces that surround her. But she must discover this for herself, in God's good time. My role is *to be with* her, always aware that the Holy Spirit is the real spiritual director.

Prior to the Second Vatican Council, spiritual direction was available primarily to priests and religious. Indeed, it was part of their religious formation. As spiritual direction has become available to people outside religious vocations, more and more laypeople have discovered this valuable spiritual resource, and there has been a greater understanding that the spiritual journey is that of the directee and that he or she is the person ultimately responsible for growing closer to God. For the aging, spiritual direction may be particularly helpful in discerning how God is calling us to live at this stage of our lives and in looking forward to a horizon that is coming ever nearer.

Director and directee usually meet once a month, for a period of forty-five minutes to an hour, although neither the frequency nor the length of the meetings must fit any particular pattern. All that is required of the directee is a sincere desire to develop a closer relationship with God, and a commitment to regular prayer.

What is discussed in each spiritual direction session will vary according to the directee's situation. The conversation should be limited to spiritual matters; friendly chitchat can sometimes be a defense mechanism for avoiding a difficult subject. The director will usually expect to hear the most important experiences in the directee's spiritual life since they last met. Sometimes there will be one overriding experience; at other times, there may be a pattern of recurring themes or no pattern at all. Keeping a spiritual journal and reviewing it before meeting the director can be useful in prayerfully preparing for the meeting, but doing so is not mandatory. The director may be helpful in discerning consolations and desolations and may sometimes suggest a specific form of prayer or a Scripture passage for meditation. Whether to follow the suggestion is entirely up to the directee, and a good director will never inquire whether the directee did so.

Above all, both director and directee should strive for greater awareness of the presence of the Holy Spirit, in their spiritual conversations and in their lives.

The first question people often ask is how to find a spiritual director. There are several answers, depending on various factors, such as region of the country. There are no uniform standards for spiritual directors; anyone can hang out a shingle. Unlike psychiatrists, lawyers, and hairdressers, they are not required to be licensed. The training they have received may be as different as a master's degree in theology or ministry from a Jesuit university; a university-level program leading to a certificate in spiritual direction; or a more informal course of training offered by a diocese, retreat house, or other institution.

For one seeking a director trained in Ignatian spirituality, a good place to start is a Jesuit university that offers training in spiritual direction and can refer people to its alumni. Among the institutions with well-established programs are Creighton University in Omaha, Nebraska; Fordham University in New York City; and Boston College in Chestnut Hill, Massachusetts. Their graduates may be anywhere in the world. The increasing numbers of laypeople trained in these programs have created a wide pool of talent, facilitating the search for the right match. A grandfather may be comfortable with a married deacon, while many women find a laywoman or a religious sister a better match than a priest.

The faculty of Jesuit high schools or the staff of Jesuit parishes may also be good sources of referrals. While not all Jesuits give spiritual direction, many of them are well acquainted with those who do.

Retreat houses can also be helpful. Some augment their full-time staffs in the summer, when the demand for retreats is heaviest, and may be able to refer an inquirer to one of these directors. In approaching a retreat house, however, it's important to know something of the background of the permanent staff. Some retreat houses offer opportunities for personal prayer and solitude, but their personnel are not necessarily trained or equipped to offer spiritual direction. It's best to choose an establishment where you have already made a retreat.

Parish priests may or may not be helpful. They often have extensive experience in counseling, helping people with serious problems that need immediate remedies. They rarely have time to give spiritual direction themselves and may not have many qualified spiritual directors in their Rolodexes. If you know your pastor well, it could be worth a try.

As a last resort, an online search can serve as a starting point. The Office of Ignatian Spirituality, a ministry of the Maryland and USA Northeast Provinces of the Society of Jesus, has recently started an online database.[44] Spiritual Directors International is an organization that maintains a roster of available spiritual directors—but be aware that the list is ecumenical, and the organization's definition of spiritual director is broad. Careful scrutiny of a director's biography and training is called for.[45]

The right fit between director and directee is essential. Talking about such intimate matters as the deepest desires of one's heart requires a degree of mutual trust. Despite the best intentions of both parties, it sometimes happens that a director may seem too detached or that a directee wants to focus exclusively on matters that require counseling rather than spiritual direction. It may be too difficult to set up regular appointments because the parties have incompatible schedules. In a small community, the director may be personally acquainted with many of the directee's friends or relatives, putting stress on the confidentiality of the process. Both parties need to trust their instincts on these and other signals.

As a first step, then, there should be a get-acquainted meeting, with no presuppositions. Common icebreaking questions like "What do you do?" and "Where are you from?" are as appropriate here as in other contexts, but the conversation should then proceed to a frank discussion of the director's qualifications and what the directee is seeking in spiritual direction. Some questions a prospective directee should ask may include the following:

- *Where have you trained as a spiritual director?*

  Someone trained in Benedictine or Franciscan spirituality may be a gifted spiritual director but not the right match for someone attracted to Ignatian spirituality. Conversely, as one of my teachers pointed out, not everyone who has *SJ* after his name is a qualified spiritual director. A director should be willing to summarize his or her background and experience. Reluctance or evasion is usually a red flag for the prospective directee to look elsewhere.

- *Have you any experience with directees in my age group?*

  Someone who spends most of his time with Jesuit novices may not be the best match for a layperson with children, grandchildren, and financial problems. But a prospective director shouldn't be ruled out based on age alone. I am approximately the same age as my director's mother, but he has been a channel of grace for me for a number of years.

- *Where do you meet your directees?*

  A quiet, contemplative environment free of distractions is essential. Parishes and retreat houses often have suitable conference rooms or parlors; a lay director may have an office. Public places and either party's residence should normally be avoided.

- *When are you usually available?*

  Some directors have specific days set aside for direction; those with full-time jobs may be available only in the evening; still others will be extremely flexible.

- *Do you charge for your services?*

  It sometimes surprises people that priests and religious expect payment for spiritual services, but many religious orders need income generated by their members in order to survive. Some lay directors function much as any others in the helping professions, such as therapists or counselors, with a regular fee schedule. However, many directors, both religious and lay, accept no payment. In these circumstances, the directee might consider making a generous gift, perhaps at Christmas, to a religious director's congregation or to a charity favored by a lay director. Finally, and most important: *What can I expect from you? What do you expect of me?*

The director, in turn, will have questions. The prospective directee should be prepared to describe his or her spiritual background with some particularity. Typical questions might be the following:

- Have you ever had spiritual direction before?
- What moved you to seek spiritual direction at this time?
- How do you pray?
- Who is God for you?
- What can I expect from you? What do you expect of me?

Sometimes the get-acquainted meeting ends with exchanging contact information and fixing the first appointment. More often, the director will leave it to the directee to call or e-mail. This approach avoids embarrassment if either party decides not to go forward. It also places the primary responsibility where it belongs: on the directee.

Prayer Exercise: Discernment

Choose a period of time—the past week or month, or the period since an important event, and reflect on the following questions:

Where have you met the evil spirit?

Are there trivial things that annoy you? Do you complain about them? How do they affect your relationships? Your prayer?

Are there subjects you don't want to discuss with anyone? Can you talk to God about them? Is there a closed door in your emotional environment? Can you ask Jesus to open it?

Is there something you need help with? Can you admit it? Can you ask for help? If not, can you ask Jesus for help?

Can you name your fears? Can you talk to Jesus about them?

Where have you met the Holy Spirit?

Can you quiet yourself to listen for the "tiny whispering sound"?

When you are aware of the presence of the Holy Spirit, how do you respond?

What, if anything, keeps you from being fully open to God's Spirit?

Suggested Scripture Readings

Downsizing

- Matthew 6:25–34; Luke 12:22–34 (Dependence on God)
- Matthew 25:14–30; Luke 19:12–26 (Parable of the Talents)
- Mark 12:41–44; Luke 21:1–4 (The Widow's Mite)
- Mark 10:17–31; Luke 18:18–30 ("What must I do to inherit eternal life?")

Poverty of Spirit

- Matthew 5:1–12 (The Beatitudes)

Discernment

- 1 Thessalonians 5:15–22
- 1 Kings 3:9–12

- Psalm 77:1–9 (A Soul in Desolation)
- Psalm 42:1–11 (A Soul in Desolation Remembering God's Grace)
- Psalm 34:1–8 (Spiritual Consolation)
- Psalm 131 (A Soul at Peace)

5

God Isn't Finished
with Me Yet

Inevitably the time comes when we see that the road ahead of us is much shorter than the one we have already traveled. We can give in to sadness, or we can savor the abundant graces all around us, even now.

Another Stage of the Journey

The idea of "journey" as a metaphor for human life is at least as old as Dante. His *Divine Comedy* begins,

> Midway on our life's journey, I found myself
> In dark woods, the right road lost.

Like Dante, many writers and thinkers have focused on middle age as a time of crisis, change, and self-discovery. There is a vast popular literature on midlife crisis as well as articles and publications directed to psychologists and other professionals. Even Cicero's classic *De Senectute (On Old Age)*, written in the century before Christ, has recently been published in a modern translation subtitled *Ancient Wisdom for the Second Half of Life*. The Australian theologian Gerald O'Collins popularized the term *second journey* to describe these experiences. He cites the stories of Ignatius, St. Teresa of Calcutta, Dietrich Bonhoeffer, and the disciples on the road to Emmaus, among others, as examples of sudden changes of direction in midlife that led to profound spiritual growth.[46]

If we use the metaphor of journey, there is no reason to divide it into only two parts. Shakespeare, of course, described seven ages of man, although he found little to aspire to in any of them. O'Collins refers in passing to the possibility of "one last journey" at the end of life. Whatever the divisions, the boundaries are often indistinct. On the spiritual journey, there are many detours and wrong turns, and we sometimes seem to be caught in an endless roundabout. Those of us who have left middle age behind but are not in Shakespeare's "second childishness and mere oblivion" are in another stage of the journey. I invite you to consider its potential for grace by looking at where we have come from and where we are going.[47]

Looking Back

No matter how old we are or how we have lived, we all have some "unfinished business." There are disappointments that still hurt: the couple who couldn't have children; the manager who was downsized from a satisfying job. There are missed opportunities that we recognize only with the wisdom of maturity, "the road not taken," in Robert Frost's phrase. There are old hurts and resentments that still burn.

We cannot change the past, but we can mine it for spiritual wisdom. As a way into the graces to which our memory may lead, I suggest a variation on the *examen*, covering not one day but a longer period. A retreat is an optimal setting for this exercise, but it can be done whenever you have an uninterrupted period of quiet.

Ask the Holy Spirit for guidance in choosing a period of time to focus on. You may want to start from the last major transition in your life or go further back. The period can be long or short—whatever seems right to you. I usually try to do this on New Year's Day, looking back over the preceding year.

Next, focus on feelings and memories. Each person's life story will present different questions, but some examples are as follows:

- Of all that happened in that period, for what am I most grateful?

- Have I expressed my gratitude to the people involved? To God? Can I do that now? *Often, the people who have been instruments of grace for us are no longer with us, but we can hold them in our hearts as we thank God for them.*

- What are the most powerful emotions that surface as I look back?

- What gave rise to joy, anger, disappointment?

- Did these emotions spring from an action, an event, or an attitude of mind or heart that prevailed at that time?

- Which ones led me to God, and which ones led me away?

- Can the memory of these feelings lead me to God in the present?

- Are there emotional doors that were closed in the past that I can open now?

- How can the wisdom of the present illumine my understanding of the past?

The answers to these questions will often lead naturally to the next:

- For what do I need forgiveness?
- Is there someone, living or dead, whose forgiveness I need to ask?
- Is there someone I need to forgive for past hurts, trivial or serious?
- Can I forgive myself for missed opportunities or mistakes or the persistence of negative feelings?
- Has God forgiven me?
- Have I asked God's forgiveness?

Finally, ask God for the grace to look forward in hope.

Looking Ahead

At some point in the aging process, we confront financial planning, estate planning, health-care proxies, and other matters that look to the end of life and beyond. It can be difficult to deal with these things; some people postpone taking action precisely because doing so involves thinking about death. Ignatius's rules for decision making and discernment, discussed in the previous chapters, can be helpful here. Following are some suggestions to pray about:

- A health-care proxy and a living will can relieve the anguish of a loved one who might be called upon to make difficult decisions.

- People who have no close relatives also need someone to make decisions for them if they cannot. Is there a friend who knows and shares your values about end-of-life care? If he or she is willing to be named as your health-care proxy, you are more likely to receive care in accordance with your own values and wishes than if the decisions are left to doctors and nurses.

- Pre-planning of funerals and burial arrangements saves money and reduces stress on survivors who would otherwise have to make these decisions on short notice, with little time for research.

- Thoughtful estate planning can reduce the possibility of quarrels or animosity among children or grandchildren, especially in large or blended families or where some children or grandchildren have special needs.

- Even people with few assets should have a will, especially if they have no immediate family. A friend of mine, a psychologist who worked with developmentally disabled adults, used up most of her savings during a long illness. She steadfastly refused to make a will on the grounds that "I don't have an estate." When she died, the few thousand dollars in her bank account went by default to the State of New York. It wasn't much money, but it could have been put to better use helping the people to whom she had devoted her entire career.

But what about our spiritual legacy? Have our loved ones, our friends, and those whose lives we may have touched without realizing it experienced grace because of us? My immigrant grandparents died when I was in my late teens. I often think of questions I wish I had asked them. Children and teenagers growing up today have an unparalleled facility with audio and video technologies that can lend themselves to oral history projects. Tell them your stories.

Can you share your spiritual journey? For some people, the feelings they share with Jesus are too intimate to be shared with anyone else. For others, there may be some insights that are so powerful they cry out to be shared. It isn't necessary to preach to your friends and family about what you have learned. But don't overlook opportunities to share your story.

Living in the Present

As we age, especially in the later years, it can be all too easy to focus on the past and to think of the future in terms of planning for death. But we are alive in the present, and no matter how long or short our life span, we live our spiritual life in the present. Prayer, always a constant in a God-centered life, can become ever richer with the experience of years.

Ministry of Prayer. Whether or not we are engaged in active ministry, some of us may have the time and space to develop a more contemplative attitude. Thomas Clarke, SJ, has argued for a ministry of intercessory prayer:

> If intercession, then, is the name of the game, I believe that the group best fitted to lead it is the world's elders. We qualify for that role not through our wisdom or even through our prophetic gifts, if we have them, but through our special brand of poverty. In generational terms, it is we who are the *anawim*—the poor—through whom God works wonders. However reduced in physical, mental, emotional powers, and whether we are still "active" or "retired," we can model for all that intercessory offering of "prayers, works, joys and sufferings" through which the world is graced.[48]

Fr. Clarke is not advocating a passive attitude of prayer as a substitute for an active life. Rather, he is inviting those impoverished in the ways particular to old age to claim their place in the communion of saints, as active instruments of grace for all the people in their lives and many they will never know. In the words of the popular hymn, "The Lord hears the cry of the poor."

Praying through the Pain. Anyone who has ever tried to read the Bible or use a popular prayer app while recovering from surgery or undergoing chemotherapy can describe how difficult it is to pray in these circumstances. The words swim on the page; the meanings don't register; the mind wanders; the pain blots out all other thoughts; when the pain subsides, drowsiness takes over; some passages trigger worries and anxieties; the joyful ones seem irrelevant.

At first glance, Ignatius seems an unlikely guide to prayer in such circumstances. As a soldier, he prided himself on not showing any sign of pain and, for a period after his conversion, he was drawn to extreme penances.[49] Where his wisdom speaks to the aging, and particularly the suffering aging, is in the overriding objective of modeling ourselves after Jesus.

To know, love, and follow Jesus means experiencing pain as Jesus experienced it. In reading the Passion narratives and about the post-resurrection appearances of Jesus, applying the principles of imaginative prayer or *lectio divina* may show us how to let go of our fears and lead us to a new experience of hope. Or, as Jesus told the disciples at the Last Supper, "Where I am going you know the way" (John 14:4).

Death as Part of Life

The early Christians had a much deeper appreciation of the continuity of earthly life and life eternal. For St. Paul, the disciples who had died after seeing the risen Jesus had merely "fallen asleep" (1 Corinthians 15:6). For his and the immediately succeeding generations, martyrdom was an imminent threat. St. Perpetua, imprisoned in Carthage around AD 202, wrote of a dream of heaven in which a deacon of her community called out to her, "Perpetua, come, we are waiting for you."[50] Those who faced martyrdom, or who knew the stories of those who had experienced it, identified with the death and Resurrection of Jesus as the meaning of the Christian life. For them, the Resurrection was not merely a proof of Jesus' divinity or a fact to celebrate at Easter; it was a promise of eternal life that was as real as the Christian's life on earth.

In modern times, we have lost that sense of the continuity of earthly and eternal life. The martyrs' stories—so long ago in such a different world—have no immediacy for us. Where cancer and terrorism are more immediate threats than dying for the faith, there is little feeling of connection with the martyrs. Even those listed in the Roman Canon (now Eucharistic

Prayer I) are rarely invoked, since at least in the United States the shorter forms of the Eucharistic Prayer are much more common. In a secular society where belief in the afterlife is a minority view, we keep our thoughts to ourselves.

Although Ignatius prescribes a meditation on hell for the First Week and includes among the criteria for decision making the advice that we imagine ourselves "at the point of death" or "on judgment day," he has little explicit advice on how one should look on death.[51] This is not surprising, since his expectation was that the Exercises would most often be made by young people making decisions about their state of life.[52] For those of us who are long past such milestones, it is significant that a person making the full Exercises spends the entire second half of the experience meditating on the passion and Resurrection of Jesus. While anyone, at any stage of life, can experience abundant grace meditating on the passion and Resurrection of our Lord, these mysteries can be particularly consoling to those who are aware that the time remaining on their spiritual journey is diminishing.

In the previous chapter, I mentioned my experience meditating on the women at the foot of the cross, deep in sorrow because they did not know about the Resurrection. We don't know when or how our own stories will end, but we do know how the story of Jesus ended. Instead of looking backward toward what has been lost or given up, we can ask for the grace to look forward with hope to life eternal, remembering the promise of Jesus: "I will see you again and your hearts will rejoice and no one will take your joy away from you" (John 16:22).

Ignatian Prayer: Suscipe

At the end of the Spiritual Exercises, Ignatius prescribes the following prayer, usually called the *suscipe,* from the first word in the Latin version:

> Take, Lord, and receive all my liberty, my memory, my understanding, and all my will—all that I have and possess. You, Lord, have given all that to me. I now give it back to you, O Lord. All of it is yours. Dispose of it according to your will. Give me your love and your grace, for that is enough for me.[53]

This kind of surrender is vastly different from giving up material goods. I have often wondered whether the middle-aged Ignatius had any inkling of the reaction this prayer might evoke in someone whose liberty was circumscribed by declining health, whose short-term memory was fading, and who was worrying about loss of understanding and will in the event of dementia. I venture to suggest that people in their seventies and eighties might have a fuller grasp of the magnitude of this prayer than a young person choosing a state in life.

Can a person confined to a nursing home after a stroke or an accident freely and sincerely ask God to "take . . . my liberty"? What about surrendering my understanding? It is no surprise that some people find this prayer difficult or impossible. But even for those of us who have difficulty with consenting to the diminishment that comes with age, the words of the suscipe are a reminder that everything is God's gift: every breath we take, every beat of our hearts, every memory we cherish, every thought that fills our minds. God may not be asking us to give up any of these gifts, just yet. But as we grow older, we should be able to be more grateful for all the graces God has showered upon us and never cease to thank and praise God every day of our lives. When we are asked to surrender, the grace will be there.

Suggested Scripture Readings

- John 14:1–7
- John 21:18
- Revelation 21:1–3
- Passion narratives: Matthew 26:1–27:61; Mark 14:17–15:47; Luke 22:31–23:55; John 18:1–19:45

- Post-resurrection appearances: John 18:1–19:45; Mark 16:1–8, 9–19; Luke 24:1–51; John 20:1–21:23; Acts 1:3–9; 1 Corinthians 15:5–8

Ignatian Resources

The literature on Ignatian spirituality is vast. Sources I have drawn on or quoted are cited in the Endnotes. Rather than a comprehensive bibliography, I offer the following suggestions that may be of particular interest to the aging.

Ignatian Spirituality

David L. Fleming, SJ, *What Is Ignatian Spirituality?* (Chicago: Loyola Press, 2008).

James Martin, SJ, *The Jesuit Guide to (Almost) Everything: A Spirituality for Real Life* (New York: HarperCollins, 2010).

The Examen

Jim Manney, *A Simple Life-Changing Prayer: Discovering the Power of St. Ignatius Loyola's Examen* (Chicago: Loyola Press, 2011).

Mark E. Thibodeaux, SJ, *Reimagining the Ignatian Examen: Fresh Ways to Pray from Your Day* (Chicago: Loyola Press, 2015).

Lectio Divina

Rev. Fr. Gabriel Mestre, *Pray with the Bible, Meditate with the Word: The Exciting World of Lectio Divina* (Philadelphia: American Bible Society, 2011).

Imaginative Prayer

James Martin, SJ, *Jesus: A Pilgrimage* (New York: HarperCollins, 2014).

Henri J. M. Nouwen, *The Return of the Prodigal Son: A Story of Homecoming* (New York: Doubleday, 1994).

Historical Fiction

Geraldine Brooks, *The Secret Chord* (New York: Viking, 2016). (The story of King David, narrated by the prophet Nathan).

Taylor Caldwell, *Dear and Glorious Physician* (New York: Doubleday, 1959). (The story of St. Luke).

Taylor Caldwell, *Great Lion of God* (1970). (The story of St. Paul).

Anne Rice, *Christ the Lord: Out of Egypt* (New York: Ballantine Books, 2008). (The childhood of Jesus).

Films

Ben Hur (1959).

Jesus of Nazareth (1977). (Franco Zeffirelli's television miniseries, now available on DVD).

The Red Tent (2014). (Based on the story of Dinah, daughter of Jacob and Leah).

The Young Messiah (2016). (Based on Anne Rice's book *Christ the Lord: Out of Egypt*).

The Spiritual Exercises

The full Exercises are not a book to be read but a set of guidelines for spiritual directors. Listed here are some offshoots and adaptations that may be of interest to those who are unable to make the substantial commitment of time and solitude required for the full Exercises.

Online Retreats

"A 34-Week Retreat for Everyday Life" (guides for daily prayer and extensive resources, including help for groups; available in many languages as well as audio format):

http://onlineministries.creighton.edu/
CollaborativeMinistry/cmo-retreat.html.

Andy Alexander, SJ, Maureen McCann Waldron, and Larry
Gillick, SJ, *Retreat in the Real World: Finding Intimacy
with God Wherever You Are* (Chicago: Loyola Press,
2009). (Paperback version of the Creighton University
34-Week Retreat).

"An Ignatian Prayer Adventure" (an eight-week adapted
version of the Spiritual Exercises):
http://www.ignatianspirituality.com/ignatian-prayer/
the-spiritual-exercises/an-ignatian-prayer-adventure/.

John E. Sassani and Mary Ann McLaughlin, *Meeting Christ
in Prayer* (Chicago: Loyola Press, 2008). (An eight-week
program designed for parish group use).

Life of St. Ignatius Loyola

The translation of the *Autobiography of St. Ignatius Loyola* by
Parmananda R. Divarkar, SJ, is an often-cited English
version. Many other translations are available, with and
without notes, e.g., James Brodrick, SJ, *St. Ignatius Loyola,
the Pilgrim Years, 1491–1538* (San Francisco: Ignatius Press,
1998); Pierre Emonet, SJ, *Ignatius of Loyola: Legend and
Reality*, ed. Thomas M. McCoog, SJ, trans. Jerry Ryan
(Philadelphia: St. Joseph's University Press, 2016).

Endnotes

1. Ignatian Volunteer Corps, 112 E. Madison Street, Baltimore, MD 21202, www.ivcusa.org.

2. Cabrini Immigrant Services of NYC, 139 Henry Street, New York, NY 10002, http://www.cis-nyc.org.

3. A more staid biblical version is found in Proverbs 16:9.

4. Jesuit Volunteer Corps, 801 Saint Paul Street, Baltimore, MD 21202.

5. Mercy Associates, 8380 Colesville Road, #300, Silver Spring, MD 20910, https://www.sistersofmercy.org/contact-us/#become-an-associate.

6. L'Arche USA, 1130 SW Morrison Street, Suite 230, Portland, OR 97205, https://www.larcheusa.org.

7. Statistics and projections on aging and life expectancy are from the 2016 Report of the Federal Interagency Forum on Aging Related Statistics, available at https://agingstats.gov, or in print form from the U.S. Government Publishing Office. The New England Centenarian Study, under the auspices of Boston University Medical School, estimates the number of centenarians at more than 80,000 and argues that "the older you get, the healthier you've been." http://www.bumc.bu.edu/centenarian/overview.

8. Retreat in Daily Life, Spiritual Exercises based on Annotation 19; the simplified version is based on Annotation 18.

9. See SpEx 23 (Principle and Foundation).

10. Margaret Silf, *Simple Faith* (Chicago: Loyola Press, 2012), 31–32.

11. George Aschenbrenner, "Consciousness Examen," *Review for Religious* 31, (1972), 14–21.

12. Aschenbrenner suggests beginning with the prayer for enlightenment but notes that the first two steps are interchangeable.

13. Michelangelo's *Rondanini Pietà*, left unfinished, is in the Castello Sforzesco in Milan, Italy. Their English-language Web site is at https://www.milanocastello.it/en.

14. "[U]nchangeable elections": SpEx 172; "changeable": SpEx 173; "either indifferent or good": SpEx 170; "God our Lord moves and attracts the will . . . ": SpEx 175.

15. Rational way of proceeding: SpEx 178–183.

16. Richard J. Hauser, SJ, *Moving in the Spirit: Becoming a Contemplative in Action* (Mahwah, NJ: Paulist Press, 1986), 70.

17. SpEx 179.

18. SpEx 183. See commentators, e.g., Richard J. Hauser, SJ, *Moving in the Spirit: Becoming a Contemplative in Action* (Mahwah, NJ: Paulist Press, 1986), 76–79; Dean Brackley, *The Call to Discernment in Troubled Times* (New York: Crossroad Publishing Company, 2004), 151.

19. SpEx 135.

20. SpEx 214.

21. SpEx 112.

22. Museum databases: For example, the Google Cultural Institute has a growing database, already in the millions of images, including hundreds by Michelangelo, Raphael, and other Renaissance artists known for their religious imagery, https://www.google.com/culturalinstitute. A collaborative effort among fourteen art institutions, known as Pharos, has created a searchable database that will eventually hold seventeen million artworks as well as supplemental material. Ted Loos, "'Photo Archives Are Sleeping Beauties.' Pharos Is Their Prince." *New York Times*, March 14, 2017, https://www.nytimes.com/2017/03/14/arts/design/art-history-digital-archive-museums-pharos.html. See also www.pharosartresearch.org. Individual museums such as the Metropolitan Museum of Art in New York and the National Gallery in London have their own searchable online databases.

23. My questions were suggested by *The Adoration of the Shepherds* by Guido Reni (1575–1642). The original is in the National Gallery, London. https://www.nationalgallery.org.uk/paintings/guido-reni-the-adoration-of-the-shepherds.

24. Advice on property: SpEx 155, 166; on spending: 189; preference for poverty: 167; providing for the poor: 189.

25. Meditation on the Beatitudes: SpEx 161, 278. The Jerusalem Bible, the first English translation approved after the Second Vatican Council, is approved by the Bishops' Council of England and Wales for liturgical use.

26. "Poor in spirit": NAB, Notes to Matthew 5:3; James Martin, SJ, *Jesus: A Pilgrimage* (New York: HarperCollins, 2014), 173. Scripture scholars differ as to whether the Beatitudes describe a present reality or instead promise rewards in eternal life. The differing interpretations are discussed in James Martin, SJ, *The*

Jesuit Guide to (Almost) Everything: A Spirituality for Real Life
(New York: HarperCollins, 2010), 170–71.

27. "Motions of the heart": *Autobiography*, 6. Richard Hauser, SJ, uses
the phrase *fluctuations of the heart* in his course Discernment of
Spirits at Creighton University Graduate School of Theology.

28. Parmananda R. Divarkar, SJ, *A Pilgrim's Testament: The Memoirs
of Saint Ignatius of Loyola* (1983), 6–8.

29. George E. Ganss, ed., *Ignatius of Loyola: Spiritual Exercises and
Selected Works* (Mahwah, NJ: Paulist Press, 1991), 71.

30. Ibid.

31. Ibid.

32. Among the many discussions of broader definitions of "evil
spirits" and "good spirits," see e.g., Timothy M. Gallagher,
O.M.V., *The Discernment of Spirits: An Ignatian Guide for
Everyday Living* (New York: Crossroad Publishing Company,
2005), 33–34; Katherine Dyckman, Mary Garvin, and Elizabeth
Liebert, *The Spiritual Exercises Reclaimed: Uncovering Liberating
Possibilities for Women* (Mahwah, NJ: Paulist Press, 2001),
251–52.

33. Spiritual desolation: SpEx 317; "characteristic of the evil spirit":
SpEx 315.

34. Characteristics of clinical depression: Centers for Disease Control,
"Depression Is Not a Normal Part of Growing Older" (2017),
https://www.cdc.gov/aging/mentalhealth/depression.htm;
National Alliance on Mental Illness, "Depression in Older
Persons Fact Sheet" (2017). The CDC estimates the prevalence of
clinical depression in the elderly as between 1 and 5 percent,
whereas NAMI estimates it may be as much as 18.5 percent.

35. John Beevers, trans., *The Autobiography of Saint Thérèse of Lisieux: The Story of a Soul* (New York: Doubleday, 1957), 116–18, 136.

36. Thomas R. Nevin, *Thérèse of Lisieux: God's Gentle Warrior* (New York: Oxford University Press, 2006), 312.

37. Beevers, trans., *The Autobiography of Saint Thérèse of Lisieux*, 140.

38. Spiritual consolation: SpEx 316; "store up new strength": 319.

39. "[S]ufficient clarity and knowledge": SpEx 176.

40. Metaphors: SpEx 325–327. The "spoiled child" translation of SpEx 325 appears in David L. Fleming, SJ, *Draw Me into Your Friendship: A Literal Translation and a Contemporary Reading of the Spiritual Exercises* (Boston: Institute of Jesuit Sources, 1996), 257, and is discussed in James Martin, SJ, *The Jesuit Guide to (Almost) Everything: A Spirituality for Real Life* (New York: HarperCollins, 2010), 333.

41. SpEx 332.

42. Avoiding decisions in time of desolation: SpEx 318; recommended responses: SpEx 320–321; 323–324.

43. I have paraphrased and significantly shortened the oft-quoted definition of spiritual direction in William A. Barry and William J. Connelly, *The Practice of Spiritual Direction*, rev. ed. (New York: HarperCollins, 2009), 8: "help given by one believer to another that enables the latter to pay attention to God's personal communication to him or her, to respond to this personally communicating God, to grow in intimacy with this God, and to live out the consequences of the relationship."

44. Office of Ignatian Spirituality online database:
    http://www.jesuitseastois.org/
    spiritualdirection?PAGE=DTN-20170523013142.

45. Spiritual Directors International: PO Box 3584, Bellevue, WA
    98009; http://www.sdiworld.org.

46. Dante, *The Inferno of Dante: A New Verse Translation*, trans.
    Robert Pinsky (New York: Farrar, Straus and Giroux, 1994), lines
    1–3; Cicero, *How to Grow Old: Ancient Wisdom for the Second
    Half of Life*, trans. Philip Freeman (Princeton, NJ: Princeton
    University Press, 2016); Gerald O'Collins, *The Second Journey:
    Spiritual Awareness and the Mid-Life Crisis* (Mahwah, NJ: Paulist
    Press, 1978), 38–40 (Ignatius); 46 (Mother Teresa); 40–42
    (Dietrich Bonhoeffer); 81 (disciples). His "third journey"
    encompasses "aging and the last years before death," which he
    sees as consisting of "beauty and simplicity," in part because of
    the "comforting advantage" of the company of "millions of fellow
    travelers," 12–14.

47. William Shakespeare, *As You Like It*, act II, scene 7, lines
    139–166. In middle age, he sees one "in fair round belly, with
    good capon lin'd . . . full of wise saws" who next "shifts into the
    lean and slippered pantaloon with spectacles on nose and pouch
    at side," lines 154–156.

48. Thomas E. Clarke, SJ, "Elderhood for the World," *America* (July
    29, 2000), 9.

49. Not showing any sign of pain: *Autobiography*, 2; extreme
    penances: 14–17.

50. Perpetua's vision: Herbert Musurillo, trans., *The Acts of the
    Christian Martyrs* (New York: Oxford University Press, 1972),

117. The text of "The Martyrdom of Saints Perpetua and Felicitas" is one of the earliest primary sources about the lives of the martyrs. Perpetua is believed to have kept a diary while imprisoned, and her story was continued by an unknown editor after her death. The narrator described how Perpetua and her companions "marched from the prison to the amphitheatre joyfully as though they were going to heaven, with calm faces, trembling, if at all, with joy rather than fear" and viewing martyrdom as "a second baptism." The full text is available online at a number of sites, e.g., https://www.scribd.com/document/ 249295097/Musurillo-Acts-of-the-Christian-Martyrs.

51. Meditation on hell: SpEx 67–82; "at the point of death": 186; "judgment day": 187.

52. Decisions about state of life: SpEx 169, 171–172.

53. Suscipe prayer: SpEx 234.

Acknowledgments

My thanks to James Martin, SJ, for his support and encouragement throughout this project; to Dr. Eileen Burke-Sullivan, who suggested the article that eventually grew into this book; to the team at Loyola Press: Joseph Durepos, Vinita Wright, Becca Russo, and Yvonne Micheletti; to Rebecca Pearson for a photograph that is "really me"; and, above all, to the people who shared their stories with me.

About the Author

Barbara Lee is a practicing spiritual director, a graduate of the Christian Spirituality Program at the Creighton University Graduate School of Theology. After a career as an attorney and a U. S. Magistrate Judge, she took early retirement and joined the Ignatian Volunteer Corps, an organization of retired people who do volunteer work among the poor in the context of Ignatian Spirituality. In 2011, she received the New York Region's Della Strada Award for "a lifetime committed to love in deeds of service transforming the world with true zeal." Her other volunteer work has included teaching English at an immigrant services center and serving in organizations working to promote Christian unity. She lives in New York City.

Other Ignatian Titles

What Is Ignatian Spirituality?

DAVID FLEMING, SJ

ENGLISH I 2718-9 I PB I $12.95
SPANISH I 3883-3 I PB I $12.95

Hearts on Fire
Praying with Jesuits

MICHAEL HARTER, SJ

2120-3 I PB I $12.95

A Simple, Life-Changing Prayer
Discovering the Power of St. Ignatius Loyola's Examen

JIM MANNEY

ENGLISH I 3535-1 I PB I $9.95
SPANISH I 4389-9 I PB I $9.95

Reimagining the Ignatian Examen
Fresh Ways to Pray from Your Day

MARK E. THIBODEAUX, SJ

ENGLISH I 4244-1 I PB I $12.95
SPANISH I 4512-1 I PB I $12.95

To Order:

Call **800.621.1008**, visit **loyolapress.com/store**, or visit your local bookseller.

Other Ignatian Titles

Ignatian Spirituality A to Z

JIM MANNEY

4598-5 | PB | $14.95

What's Your Decision?
How to Make Choices with Confidence and Clarity

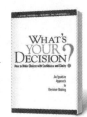

SPAROUGH ET AL.

3148-3 | PB | $10.95

The Ignatian Adventure
Experiencing the Spiritual Exercises of St. Ignatius in Daily Life

KEVIN O'BRIEN, SJ

ENGLISH | 3577-1 | PB | $14.95
SPANISH | 4520-6 | PB | $14.95

An Ignatian Book of Days

JIM MANNEY

4145-1 | PB | $12.95

To Order:

Call **800.621.1008**, visit **loyolapress.com/store**, or visit your local bookseller.

Ignatian Spirituality

www.ignatianspirituality.com

Visit us online to

- Join our E-Magis newsletter
- Pray the Daily Examen
- Make an online retreat with the *Ignatian Prayer Adventure*
- Participate in the conversation with the dotMagis blog and at **facebook.com/ignatianspirituality**